G000123383

THE LIFELINE

Martin Scott

Explorations in Theology

- volume four -

Boz Publications Ltd.

71-75 Shelton Street - Covent Garden - London - WC2H 9JQ - United Kingdom.

office@bozpublications.com / www.bozpublications.com

BOZ PUBLICATIONS

Copyright © 2021 Martin Scott

First published 2021 by Boz Publications Ltd

ISBN: 978-1-8384003-3-0

A CIP catalogue record for this book is available from the British Library.

Contents

PREFACE

A RECAP AND AN APOSTOLIC OBJECTION

I have sought to write these small volumes in a way that builds from one to the next. I do not suggest that I have chosen the best path, nor one that could not be contradicted. In the opening book ('Humanising the Divine') two important principles were suggested that started the trajectory. The first is that through God's gracious choice, and creative act, there is not a great chasm between humanity and the divine. Created in the image of God, humanity's call is to represent God within material creation. Although, for me, the jury is out whether there is a historic and literal fall or the story belongs to myth (Genesis 3, and by extension Genesis 3-11), the verdict it presents is that humanity has indeed fallen short of being what they were intended to become. They have fallen short of the glory of God, and in that first volume I suggest we can substitute the term 'failed to be(come) truly human', to describe this falling short. That concept was something I considered was a succinct description of the core issue that we term 'sin', namely to fall short of the glory of God.

The second principle that I presented there was that only Jesus is the one who shows what it is to be truly human. At no stage in his life does he sin, but being born as a first-century Jew, his environment was one with a bias that marginalised non-Jews and women.

Although sinless, he became mature through what he suffered, and at numerous stages in his development faced some challenges, particularly when he is in the context of non-Jews and women, to go beyond his contextual bias and respond as one who is truly human. That response provoked him to reach beyond his immediate world that excluded others. By the final Easter when he was crucified he was indeed mature and thus was to become the source of salvation to all. He becomes that source as a truly mature human (Heb. 5:8, 9). We can conclude that the cross is indeed an accurate revelation of God, the place and time where God's glory is fully revealed. God is the God who embraces human suffering.

There was one other aspect that comes through in that first volume, namely that any theory of the atonement has to take into account the 'when' of the cross; indeed the 'when' will strongly influence the answer sought to the 'what' is accomplished at the cross. Too much of traditional theology jumps to a theory concerning the 'what' without ever answering the 'when' question. The cross occurred at the 'fullness of times' (Gal. 4:4; Rom. 5:6), the time when there was no hope for humanity to find a way back to the path of true humanness, when the bondage over the nations (including the 'nation' of Israel) was at a fullness.

The Jewish context was one of compromise, thus through their insistence on having a king so that they might be as one of the nations, they had, by the time of Jesus, no king other than Caesar. With Israel in bondage the blessing to the nations could not be released. In that very real sense Jesus' death was first for the Jew, then for the Gentiles.

The second book ('Significant Other') explored the call on the church/body of Christ / Jesus' partner as a political movement. Jesus finished his task, but there remained a task to be completed. That task was the commission of the *ekklesia* on behalf of the world. A political task, not political in the sense of being aligned to a specific political ideology, but carrying a vision for the future of the world, living life from the future, and carrying responsibility for the nations - the world that lay beyond the boundaries of 'the people of God'. The call on Israel to be 'a royal priesthood' being the paradigm that I used to take this trajectory forward. Using the common ('secular') usage of the word 'ekklesia' I then put forward that this was indeed what Paul was planting in each of the cities and regions that he worked in.

As an apostle Paul carried a global vision. Jesus had broken compromised religious power in Jerusalem, where this was centred, so that Paul (and the subsequent *ekklesia*) could carry the message of the crucified Messiah to the centre of the then one-world-government, Rome. The huge vision, the total transformation of this world into something that God sees for humanity is so big that one might easily conclude that a participation in this vision would be restricted to 'big' people, those particularly gifted and powerful. However, the reverse is the case, with Paul stating that God has chosen those who 'are not' to confound that which is! In Volume 3 ('A Subversive Movement') I follow that theme.

The whole Jesus project is quite remarkable. Here we have a first-century Jew with what we term 'the Old Testament' as his guide (and a few other books that were eventually not considered Scripture by Jews or Christians), growing up with certain perspectives that his world view would have given him. To suggest he was radical would be an understatement, and his lack of popularity among religious leaders naturally followed his radicality. They might have been intrigued by him and unable to shake him off, but he was never going to be voted into a 'hall of fame' by such leaders! He was the great Teacher because he was the great Learner, and as such broke out of all the narrow-minded perspectives his immediate world sought to shape him by. Then beyond Jesus, it is remarkable that, in the context of an all-but one-world-domination, a message, formed among a minority of irrelevant middle-eastern people, that what happened through the crucifixion of this one individual had cosmic implications, went on to impact the then known world.[1]

So now we arrive at this volume! Time to drill a little deeper into Paul's Gospel as he expressed it and to consider what the implications could be. The Gospel message is a lifeline thrown to humanity to be pulled on, enabling us to avoid the seemingly inevitable path that only leads to a fundamentally self-made destruction. It is a lifeline drawn by the finger of heaven in the dust of humanity. Humanity chose to draw a different line, the line of right and wrong; religion sharpened this, thus dividing humanity; the Gospel re-establishes the original line, calling us to come over to the life side, experiencing life and becoming a life source.

Objectionable apostle?

Galatians is one of the earliest of writings that we have, in what has become the canon of the New Testament. In it, Paul is blunt and to the point as he defends the simplicity of the Gospel that he received from heaven (Galatians 1:12). He states it succinctly in the opening verses of the first chapter, where we read, '[Jesus] who gave himself for our sins to rescue us from the present evil age'. Simple it might have been but the implications were, and continue to be, deeply profound. The Galatians were Gentile converts to faith in Jesus, but in Paul's absence they were being confronted by teachers who claimed that their conversion was only a 'half-way' conversion, and that they were missing the whole aspect of obedience to the Jewish

---

1 Crucifixion was not unique to Jesus. During the close of the siege of Jerusalem (AD70) the Romans were crucifying up to 500 Jews a day as a sign of their dominance. In 4BC the Roman general Varus crucified 2,000 Jews, and crucifixions were not an uncommon event within the life of the empire. This makes it all the more remarkable that the level of significance given to the death of this one Jew took hold. Then considering that it took place in an obscure colony far away from Rome and within a few years the message was having an impact on that Empire, I suggest that we are looking at a truly spectacular phenomenon.

law, complete with circumcision.[2] They were being told that only by compliance to the Torah (Jewish law) could they be descendants of Abraham and therefore part of the family of God.

Paul's response was not very diplomatic as he did not allow for any middle ground. Those teachers were proclaiming 'a different gospel' and he invited a curse from heaven to come on them:

I am astonished that you are so quickly deserting the one
who called you to live in the grace of Christ and are turning
to a different gospel - which is really no gospel at all.
Evidently some people are throwing you into confusion
and are trying to pervert the Gospel of Christ.
But even if we or an angel from heaven should preach
a gospel other than the one we preached to you,
let them be under God's curse! As we have already said,
so now I say again: If anybody is preaching to you a gospel
other than what you accepted, let them be under God's curse!

− (Gal. 1:6-9) −

Paul's understanding of the Gospel was such that he gave no value to fulfilling the Jewish rite of circumcision. The only value he held to was that of 'new creation':

Neither circumcision nor uncircumcision means anything;
what counts is the new creation.
− (Gal. 6:15) −

---

2 Paul is defending a 'Torah-free' Gospel for these Gentile converts. It appears that many of the early believers who were Jews by birth continued to adhere to the Law (Acts 21:20). The challenge of table-fellowship was an inevitable result.

This is the same language (*kaine ktisis*: new creation) as in 2 Corinthians 5:17 where in that context he writes that for those who are in Christ how they see others has been totally altered. No one can be viewed according to any former value system, for 'if anyone is in Christ [there is] new creation'. Through Christ's death on the cross there is a new social order. Perhaps the best summary of the effect of the Gospel, the birth of this new social order is the classic summary text in Galatians 3:28, 29:

> *There is neither Jew nor Gentile, neither slave nor free,*
> *nor is there male and female, for you are all one in Christ Jesus.*
> *If you belong to Christ, then you are Abraham's seed,*
> *and heirs according to the promise.*

There are no second-class citizens, and neither are there any elite members. The result of the Gospel was a total equalisation. In the light of this we have to be careful when a community of faith develops, so that any structure that is established does not result in a hierarchy.[3]

The confrontation (in Galatians 2) that took place with Peter 'to his face' makes for interesting reading. Paul was unafraid to confront someone who was intimate with Jesus, and so incensed was Paul that he did it publicly. Maybe Paul was somewhat obnoxious, or maybe his passion for the Gospel demanded the confrontation. We read,

> *When Cephas came to Antioch,*
> *I opposed him to his face, because he stood condemned.*

---

3 Permanent structures will always tend toward some measure of hierarchy. Hierarchical structures tend to result in those who are within that structure remaining immature. This is probably why research suggests that church in its normal form can help people reach a level of maturity but then (by default) resist them growing beyond that.

For before certain men came from James,
he used to eat with the Gentiles. But when they arrived,
he began to draw back and separate himself from the
Gentiles because he was afraid of those who belonged to the
circumcision group. The other Jews joined him in his hypocrisy,
so that by their hypocrisy even Barnabas was led astray.

━ *(Gal. 2:11-13)* ━

We are not told exactly what those who came from James said that convinced Peter[4] to no longer eat with the Gentile believers, but I suggest it must have been a very convincing argument. So convincing that 'even Barnabas' followed Peter's example. Barnabas, the one who reached out to Paul when no-one else would,

When he came to Jerusalem, he tried to join the disciples,
but they were all afraid of him, not believing that he
really was a disciple. But Barnabas took
him and brought him to the apostles.

━ *(Acts 9:26,27)* ━

The same Barnabas that the Jerusalem apostles sent to Antioch to find out what was really happening there, sending him to a situation where Gentiles were supposedly responding to Jesus. He was sent, it seems, as he would discern if God was really present irrespective of any compliance with the Torah.

---

4 Paul uses Peter's Aramaic name, Cephas, maybe indicating that Peter can be a Jew if he wishes but he cannot be part of the group who want to impose Torah on the Gentiles. Peter cannot impose any personal choices on them.

*News of this reached the church in Jerusalem, and they sent
Barnabas to Antioch. When he arrived and saw
what the grace of God had done, he was glad
and encouraged them all to remain true
to the Lord with all their hearts.*

— *(Acts 11:22,23)* —

Given how generous and accepting Barnabas was we can understand Paul's use of the word 'even' when recounting his friend's behaviour. For Barnabas to draw a line and exclude people the argument must have been strong. Perhaps we get an insight into it when we read of Paul's later visit to Jerusalem and his meeting with 'James and the elders'. He first reports to them what God had done among the Gentiles, but the tangible nervousness about having Paul in the Jewish headquarters is so evident.

*When they heard this, they praised God.
Then they said to Paul: "You see, brother,
how many thousands of Jews have believed,
and all of them are zealous for the law.
They have been informed that you teach all the Jews
who live among the Gentiles to turn away from Moses,
telling them not to circumcise their children or live
according to our customs.*

What shall we do?

*They will certainly hear that you have come,
so do what we tell you. There are four men with us
who have made a vow. Take these men,
join in their purification rites and pay their expenses,*

so that they can have their heads shaved.
Then everyone will know there is no truth
in these reports about you, but that you yourself
are living in obedience to the law".

━ *(Acts 21:20-24)* ━

Paul in town certainly caused the ripples of panic to go out! The early church consisted of Jewish believers (many thousands) who continued in obedience to the law, and it was increasingly consisting of Gentile believers who did not comply with the law. The rumour was that Paul was teaching Jewish believers to turn away from compliance with the law. (Although he was not doing this, he might well have done so, except his mission was to the Gentiles!) With this Scriptural insight into the level of nervousness over Paul's presence, and that the argument of those who came from James even convinced gracious Barnabas to pull back from the Gentile Christians in Galatia, we have to come up with a suggestion that fits the outcome. I suggest that those who came from Jerusalem came with a missiological argument.

James and the elders persuade 'loose cannon' Paul not to make their lives difficult and to publicly comply with the vow-taking ritual. In the same way I consider that the strong argument that won over Peter, the other Jews and 'even' Barnabas went along similar lines. So, putting words in the mouths of those Jews, here is my take.

'If you eat with the Gentiles you will be making our lives very difficult back in Jerusalem and Judea. We have many Jews there who are followers of Jesus so what kind of message are you sending back to them if you are clearly not complying with what is required of us as Jews? This will cause nothing but confusion and set back the work of God years, and we could well end up with some of those believers losing their faith. And as far as reaching other Jews you will make it almost impossible as they will understand from your actions that they will have to deny the faith of their ancestors to follow Jesus'.

A convincing missiological / pastoral argument. It has to be something along those lines that convinced the pull-back. Paul, however, simply labels it as 'hypocrisy' and publicly rebukes Peter.

Before drawing this section to a conclusion there is one other Scripture I wish to throw into the mix. In Acts 16:1-3 we read that Paul insisted that Timothy be circumcised:

> *Paul came to Derbe and then to Lystra,*
> *where a disciple named Timothy lived, whose mother*
> *was Jewish and a believer but whose father was a Greek.*
> *The believers at Lystra and Iconium spoke well of him.*
> *Paul wanted to take him along on the journey,*
> *so he circumcised him because of the Jews who lived in that area,*
> *for they all knew that his father was a Greek.*

In the Galatian letter he is so strongly opposed to those who are insisting on circumcision being required of the Gentile converts,[5] and yet in the passage quoted above he insists on Timothy submitting to that rite. Confused?

Thankfully in the passage concerning Timothy there is a very clear reason. The reason was a missiological one, so as not to offend the audience. This accords with Paul's claim that he 'became all things to all people so that by all means he might win some'. He could act one way in one situation, and another way in another setting, but the reason for any adapted behaviour was missiological. He was willing to

---

5 'As for those agitators, I wish they would go the whole way and emasculate themselves!'. (Gal. 5:12)

compromise for the sake of the Gospel, but refused to compromise the Gospel itself. When we assess these passages where there appears to be responses that conflict with each other we should note that the relational or contextual aspect seems to influence the practice. When Paul was with the Jews in Jerusalem he was willing to go along with a ritual, but when among the Galatian Gentiles any such compliance would be nothing less than a compromise of the Gospel, it would indeed be 'another' Gospel.

It is indeed complex, and so it has to be. How we compromise for the sake of the Gospel without compromising the Gospel itself has to challenge us to the core; conversely, if we do not compromise for the sake of the Gospel we are in danger of compromising the very Gospel itself, the good news from heaven for all people and all cultures.

Here are three tentative suggestions:

- If we are communicating with those who do not profess faith, we have to move our position to be with them. We 'eat what they set before us'. We make all kinds of compromises, for the sake of the Gospel, the Gospel that begins with a huge 'God is with us'. We firmly position ourselves alongside the 'outsider' and if we cause an offence we do it to those who see themselves as 'insiders'.
- If we are with believers who hold to certain practices, as far as possible we adjust to them and their context, particularly if their behaviour is for missiological reasons. This seems to be Paul's response in Jerusalem.
- But if ever we encounter behaviour that conflicts with the universal message of acceptance for all, without hierarchy, we have to take a tough line. Paul was willing to label it hypocrisy, 'another Gospel', and even to confront someone such as Peter.

Paul was willing to compromise when among those who had not come to faith in Jesus, also at times when with believers, but if the very message of the freedom of the Gospel was at stake he would become most objectionable, regardless of who he had to confront, so that the essential egalitarian nature of the Gospel was maintained. For Paul, to be a Jew was not to be of a higher status, neither was being male to set him at a level above those who were female. The conflict in Galatians was manifest around the table, the place of eating. The table symbolised and encapsulated total equalisation; status could not count in that setting. The table also was the furniture that reminded everyone present that the One they acknowledged as Lord used that setting to wash disciples' feet, the place where he told them that there was to be no hierarchy among them.

For Paul, when anyone was in Christ there was a new creation, and there could be no way of categorising other people along gender, ethnicity nor economic lines. What counted was to be 'in Christ', and the presence of Christ among those of faith transformed everything.

CHAPTER 1

BUT THE BIBLE

The book we hold as sacred, that we respect as authoritative, is very challenging. Separated from us by centuries, written (and probably edited) over centuries, written in very different cultures to our own, inevitably means it is very difficult to interpret at times. We can, and often do, lift verses or even whole passages and apply them directly into our culture. We might even consider that such texts are timeless, and we can be so grateful for that. However, we can also make so many errors if we assume that all biblical texts are timeless. Passages fit into a historical context, the truths applied are into that context, hence some of the 'truths' might simply not be eternal truths.[1]

Our approach to the Bible then will pretty much determine our conclusions. There is so much in the Bible that is patriarchally biased, and if we do not make allowance for that bias we will inevitably end up believing that God is biased toward males. A biblical example can be seen when we read the instructions concerning how long a woman is 'unclean' following the birth of a child.

---

1 As we will see, this has to be the case with the very clear division of 'Old' and 'New' Testaments. But we have to take it further - even the letters, where we see the heart of Christian doctrine developed, were contingent. The letters to the Corinthians, for example, were precisely that. They were letters to the Corinthian Christians in their context. This is not to say there is no timeless teaching within the letters, but any theology is also applied to that situation.

> *The Lord said to Moses, 'Say to the Israelites:*
> *'A woman who becomes pregnant and gives birth to a son*
> *will be ceremonially unclean for seven days, just as she*
> *is unclean during her monthly period. On the eighth day*
> *the boy is to be circumcised. Then the woman must wait*
> *thirty-three days to be purified from her bleeding.*
> *She must not touch anything sacred or go to the sanctuary*
> *until the days of her purification are over.*
> *If she gives birth to a daughter, for two weeks*
> *the woman will be unclean, as during her period.*
> *Then she must wait sixty-six days*
> *to be purified from her bleeding...*
>
> ▬ *(Lev. 12:1-5)* ▬

Those instructions are hard to explain! Leaving aside the term 'ceremonially unclean', why the difference between how long the woman is unclean following the birth of a son and the birth of a daughter? There is, as in most ancient cultures, a bias toward male superiority, and the ancient texts of our Scriptures come from that culture and reflect the same bias.

If we have a simple approach where everything we read is inerrant and perfectly God's word (in the sense of word for word)[2] we will come to certain conclusions that will not take us in an egalitarian direction. Add to that God as 'he'; Jesus as male; Paul as incredibly restrictive to women and we conclude 'this is just how it is, but it is God's order so we need to comply'.

However...

---

2 A rather amusing situation (unless one is from Crete!) is Titus 1:12,13 where Paul affirms a quote from a poet: 'One of Crete's own prophets has said it: "Cretans are always liars, evil brutes, lazy gluttons." This saying is true.' That Scripture alone tells us that with certain texts we cannot simply take what is written there, re-quote and apply it uncritically.

Work it out

The Old Testament law has a 'tooth for tooth, an eye for an eye' approach, known as 'lex talionis', which put limits on the response to a crime, so that the punishment was limited and appropriate. That limitation ensured that the punishment was not to exceed the level of the crime. In the Torah we read that the death penalty is prescribed for certain violent (and other) crimes. Here are some examples,

Whoever strikes a man so that he dies shall be put to death.
But if he did not lie in wait for him, but God let him fall into his
hand, then I will appoint for you a place to which he may flee.
But if a man wilfully attacks another to kill him by cunning,
you shall take him from my altar, that he may die.
Whoever strikes his father or his mother shall be put to death.
Whoever steals a man and sells him, and anyone found
in possession of him, shall be put to death.
Whoever curses his father or his mother shall be put to death.

— *(Exodus 21:12-17)* **—**

Yet the response by God to the first murder was to protect the murderer! God did not comply with his own law.[3] We can only conclude that the law of God to Israel is not the 'law of God'. Indeed Jesus said as much when he said, 'you have heard... but I say to you.' The law of God points forward, and the bigger issue with such conflicting examples is to work out how we apply what we read to situations that are in a different era and context. Many biblical texts (and in particular Old Testament Scriptures) cannot simply be imposed on all other contexts.

---

3 Genesis 4:15, 'Then the Lord put a mark on Cain so that no one who found him would kill him'.

The Bible and slavery

The Bible can be, and was, used to defend slavery. Indeed, one can build a better biblical case (if by 'biblical' we mean an approach that makes a direct appeal to the texts) for slavery as a godly institution than to argue for its abolition. Those who used the Bible for the defence of slavery[4] pulled on five key points:

1. Slavery was established by God.
2. It was practised by righteous people, and God even blessed certain people by increasing their number of slaves.
3. The moral law (perhaps an inaccurate term, but what was meant by this was the law as summarised in the 10 commandments) sanctioned and regulated slavery.
4. Jesus accepted slavery and there is no record of him raising his voice against it.
5. The apostles upheld it, evidenced by the instructions they gave concerning how slaves were to behave.

It was J.B. Lightfoot in his commentary on Colossians and Philemon (published in 1875) who seems to have been the first scholar to suggest that although the Bible allowed slavery, the principles for its eventual overthrow were laid down in Paul and the Gospel. The abolitionists had to go **beyond** the text, and consider what the right response was in the light of the Gospel; they had to give consideration to the trajectory of Scripture.

Christians were involved in the abolitionist process but it was not simply something that was Christian-led. And for the Christian community there was this further major complication, namely, what the

---

4 Charles Hodge was a prominent Presbyterian theologian and principal of Princeton Theological Seminary between 1851 and 1878, and as a scholar was scathing of the abolitionist position. He said that, 'If the present course of the abolitionists is right, then the course of Christ and the apostles were wrong'. The 1835 declaration by the Presbyterian synod of West Virginia stated that abolition was a dogma contrary to 'the clearest authority of the word of God'.

Bible taught on the issue. This response to slavery is very informative on other issues, such as the discussion on the freedom for women within society (and the Christian community).[5]

Christians debated the biblical position on slavery, but essentially what brought conviction that Scripture stood on the side of the abolitionists was the perspective that the Gospel brought. The Gospel as a message of liberation was the ultimate conviction that Bible-believing Christians were right in standing for abolition. Slavery being seen as an institution that was no longer compatible with the belief that all people were equal before their creator. In the light of the Gospel, freedom meant that an appropriate outworking should take place in the sphere of social relationships, and therefore emancipation was understood to be the right course of action.[6]

When the Bible itself was interrogated beyond the words on the page there was found to be a very strong internal critique of slavery. Although at face value biblical verses seemed to endorse slavery, the overwhelming thrust of freedom and equality before God of all individuals meant that (literally) enslaving Scriptures were eventually swept aside as no longer applying in modern cultures. The bigger narrative sweep of creation to new creation proved stronger and more persuasive than the 'story' the texts seemed to clearly endorse.

This principle of the intra-canonical dialogue (or put bluntly and simply, the internal disagreements / discrepancies / contradictions) is something that is uncomfortable at times, for it means we can-

---

5 And also other pressing discussions such as same-sex marriage.

6 In the American Declaration of Independence we read, 'We hold these truths to be self-evident, that all men are created equal, that they are endowed by their Creator with certain unalienable Rights, that among these are Life, Liberty and the pursuit of Happiness'. Yet it was years before women could vote and have other rights within the culture, and years later again before segregation was rejected. It illustrates that we can easily make a (true) plea for 'all lives matter' but insist on that from a position of privilege, and in it not to realise the great inequality that persists. Accurate sight of a situation is not normally that of the already empowered.

not sweep aside contradictions, nor swiftly move to harmonise any perceived, or real, differences. This is a major principle that I consider we have to bear in mind.

An unfolding story

So much of the biblical passages are in story form. Even the majority of the first five books (the Law) are not written as a set of laws but come to us in narrative form. There are timeless truths both within certain texts and within the overall narrative but we essentially have to approach Scripture as an unfolding story rather than as a treasure trove of timeless (detached from history) truths. A model that is fairly useful as an illustration of the nature of the Bible is that of a story being told in a series of acts.[7] We could describe it like this:

Act 1 - the narratives surrounding creation communicate something of who God is. Humanity is also positioned in relation to God and the rest of creation. From this we get some indication of where the story might end.

Act 2 - the fall, or series of falls indicate what has gone wrong and what would need be put right. From chapter 3 through to chapter 11 of Genesis we gain insights into the issues that have affected the world.

Act 3 - from the call of Abraham to the work of John the Baptist; this 'act' occupies the larger part of the Old Testament and the opening scenes of the New. Clearly, contextually, Abraham (and descendants: 'Israel') are to be the solution to those first 11 chapters of Genesis, called to be agents in undoing the effects of the fall(s) and bringing creation to her fulfilment.[8]

---

7 Writers, such as N.T. (Tom) Wright, have proposed such models.

8 The OT focuses on Abraham and then the descendants of Isaac. However, Abraham also had a son named Ishmael. Perhaps we should also see something redemptive in Ishmael's line?

Act 4 - the life, work and ministry of Jesus. This has to take a central place, as Jesus is the image of the invisible God and 'Adam at last'. One caveat, though, is that even within the above statement that 'this has to take central place' we need to recall that the work and context of Jesus is into the historic setting of Israel in the era of Roman occupation and at a time when she was expressing a major fall from her calling to take responsibility for the nations. Nevertheless what Jesus taught and embodied has to be the 'lens' through which we read the whole Bible.

Unfinished Act 5 - from the Resurrection/Pentecost and the birth of the Christian community to... And for this reason this 'act' is unfinished. The Bible is not still in process of being written but the biblical story continues. Any faithful 'telling' (and by that I mean 'living out') of the biblical story must align itself to what has gone before, and yet cannot simply quote texts from another 'act' to justify current behaviour and belief. Texts can, and must, be referred to, but if used as 'proof texts' we will probably quickly become guilty of ignoring the 'non-proof' texts.

Given that we cannot simply take texts from a previous act and apply them uncritically into our part of 'Act 5' it is self-evident that we will need the help of the Holy Spirit. We find such a dynamic approach in the 'council of Jerusalem' (Acts 15). They met together to handle a formerly unknown situation, namely what would be the right response to the influx of Gentiles as followers of Jesus. Those who gathered were predominantly Jewish believers who knew their Scriptures. They certainly did not ignore what they had read and discussed many times before, but they held back on 'proof-texting' their particular position until they had heard what God was doing by the Spirit. They heard from Peter and his experience with Cornelius' household, then they listened to the amazing stories of what God was doing among the Gentiles through Paul and Barnabas. What God was evidently doing was the major influence on how they read their Scriptures. Regardless of how they had previously understood the 'restoration of David's tabernacle' (Amos 9:11), in the context of the Jerusalem Council it was quoted to explain what God was doing in saving Gentiles. The restoration was no longer understood in a literal sense, nor primarily as a Jewish event. God's activity shaped their reading.

The unfinished nature of Scripture suggests that there is indeed a trajectory from the earlier acts toward the final scene of 'a new heaven and a new earth'. This makes biblical interpretation both challenging and also liberating. Discerning where the trajectory would take them was the convincing element with regard to the emancipation of slaves; likewise with respect to gender equality. What is clear is the pull toward freedom, and away from all kinds of metaphorical slavery. This is the direction of the trajectory.[9]

Tracking with the trajectory is a journey where our eyes are opened gradually. 'The self-evident truth that all are created equal' is a wonderful statement,[10] but in spite of the clarity of the declaration those who penned those words (white males) had eyes that were blind. Slavery continued, women were not given the vote, yet all were created equal! Such was their blindness to the self-evident truth that they so clearly claimed to subscribe to. The trajectory of the declaration might have pushed for emancipation, but then (and as I write) such a declaration has to also ask the hard question about continuing systemic racism. The journey with Scripture, likewise, will continue to push us in a 'new creation' direction, and this means moving ever toward a greater level of liberation, egalitarianism, and inclusion; the push being always toward the fulfilment of the promise inherent within Genesis. Important as the beginning is,

---

9 Not a freedom to sin, yet we have to be very careful as to what we try and declare as sin. Religion quickly defines what is sin along the lines of right and wrong; the bigger distinction in Scripture is life and death. The bias is toward freedom: 'It is for freedom that Christ has set us free. Stand firm, then, and do not let yourselves be burdened again by a yoke of slavery'. (Gal. 5:1)

10 The American Declaration of Independence.

the fulfilment is not a return to the original setting, but a process that takes us from the beginning to the conclusion. We see this in the insights we get when we step back and look at the big story: a couple defined as 'male and female' become a company that cannot be numbered where there is no male and female; a garden becomes a city with trees and a river within it; a visitation from God at the close of the day becomes the divine permanent presence of God; a separation of heaven and earth becomes the union of the two. Hence everything that increasingly marks us out as more like the end of the story, rather than the beginning, has to help us find the right path. And even calling it the 'end' of the story might prove to be the wrong term. Scripture uses the word 'eschaton' of the future rather than the equally common word 'telos'. The latter term indicates a goal in the sense of destination, but this word is not used. Perhaps the 'end' (eschaton) is the end of one era and the beginning of another one.[11] Perhaps beyond the *parousia* there is scope for growth and development. We have to leave such possibilities as speculative and probably unhelpful; what remains is a vision of 'the eschaton' that can help us find an appropriate response now. Peter might have proclaimed on the day of Pentecost that 'this is that' but we are challenged by 'then (as in future, when the eschaton arrives) is now'!

---

11 Revelation is primarily a visionary book, one that uses apocalyptic language and imagery, so we have to be careful about bringing in language from there to defend a position, but maybe when the gates of the city are never shut (Rev. 21:25), and there are those who are living outside the city, we might just have an indication that there is more to happen after the 'end'.

CHAPTER 2

AND THE BIBLE

In moving away from using arbitrary texts to prove our position (with the defensive stance of 'but the Bible...') does not mean that the Scriptures become irrelevant. Far from it. However, our use will be less definitive and more along the lines of 'and the Bible seems to suggest...' Jesus said that the Scriptures testify of him (John 5:39) and if we are comfortable to use the term 'word of God' when speaking of Scripture we need to understand that what we have in book form is the word of God that points to the 'Word of God', the Person of Jesus. We have to give precedence to the revelation of God in Jesus.

The Bible bears faithful witness to this Personal revelation, and in honouring Scripture we have to hear its testimony to Jesus, rather than simply gather our texts to prove our point. It is clear that we can stop at the Scriptures and never follow the signpost, that the Scriptures are, to the Person of Jesus. This is why we need to come to Scripture with a 'Jesus-lens' recognising that some parts, by themselves, fall short of the revelation we find in Jesus. It is the overall story that relentlessly pushes us to Jesus, and we have to allow the Jesus factor, both as already revealed in the Gospel narratives and also in what we discern God is doing through the Spirit in the world.

We read the Scriptures with a Jesus-lens

We might refer to Joseph as someone God appointed to a very high position in the alien land of Egypt, and therefore propose him as a suitable role model. That is appropriate to a certain level, but with a Jesus-lens we cannot ignore that the end result of Joseph's model was enslavement of a people to the rule of Pharaoh, with Pharaoh finally owning all the land. Likewise, it cannot escape our notice that Solomon's enslavement of Israel is not an expression of God's wisdom, the gift that was given to him. When we have a Jesus-lens we cannot read the Scriptures as a 'flat-book' with all Scriptures having equal say. We have to turn up the 'volume' of the texts that faithfully and more fully testify of Christ, and turn down the 'volume' of others. Together they might make a harmony but not through simply giving each and every text or passage equal weight.

We give weight to clear teaching Scriptures

Given that so much of the Bible is narrative there are many passages that are descriptive of what was taking place. Those narrative texts might describe a healthy or an unhealthy situation; healthily they might be reflective of original promise (the creation 'act') or comply with new creation realities (reflecting the end imagery of the final 'act'); and unhealthily they might reflect the state of things due to the fall(s), even when they describe the situation among 'godly' people. At times such descriptive texts could describe a practical compromise,[1] or they might even describe a decision that was made where we might question the rightness of the outcome.[2]

---

1 Such as the circumcision of Timothy and the instruction for women to cover their heads in 1 Corinthians 11. With regard to the second example, if it is right to read it as advocating head-covering, the instruction was given to Corinth in the first century. That application is simply irrelevant to us today, while the discussion that took place remains relevant so that we can grapple with current issues.

2 Was Paul right to split with Barnabas (Acts 15:39)?

There are also **corrective** Scriptures, where, for example, Paul is correcting a certain practice. Perhaps Paul is seeking to correct a wrong practice in 1 Corinthians 11, but we would have to be very clear we understood what was being corrected before we used such corrective passages in an applied situation.[3] To insist on applying a corrective Scripture we would have to show that it was not simply temporal and contextual.

Descriptive and corrective texts then have to be handled with care and we should be slow to implement them uncritically. Paul instructed his readers to follow him as he followed Christ. It is obedience to Jesus and conformity to his way of life that takes precedence. That cannot be substituted by blind obedience to Scripture. Indeed, Scripture itself seems to invite us to enter into the debate we find within its pages. As well as descriptive and corrective Scriptures there are, for want of a better term, **teaching** Scriptures. In the context of the letters many of them will use language such as 'in Christ', or make reference to what God did in and through Jesus. Such texts have to be given greater weight than the other two categories I have described.

By way of example, all of the texts relating to supposed restrictions on women in the Pauline writings are in the context of correction. I consider it would be a major mistake to begin with those if we were seeking to establish what the Gospel teaches about women. We would actually be better off simply responding with an agnostic response about such texts as they do not refer to here and now but to there and then. That is not to say that there is no teaching element within them, but it is to insist that any corrective element had a local and temporal element to it.

---

3 It is also interesting that Paul did not advocate any restriction on women in this passage. They could participate equally alongside the men. In participating equally there seems to be a requirement to participate in a culturally appropriate way. We cannot actually read this text as restrictive.

We do not mistake compromise
(for the sake of the Gospel) with the Gospel

There are corrective Scriptures (as mentioned above) that are often best understood as suggesting a compromise as the best way ahead at that time in a particular situation. As mentioned, the issue of head-covering that Paul addresses in 1 Corinthians 11 is probably well understood as one such example. There are descriptive texts that likewise describe a compromise; texts such as the one quoted earlier concerning the circumcision of Timothy is easily understood to fit this pattern. The reason for the compromise (invariably missiological) might help us understand the nature of the Gospel but the practice that is described should not be taken to be the Gospel practice.

In the same way the 'household codes'[4] cannot be taken as texts that are to be understood as eternal truth delivered once for all time! Household codes were part of ancient culture and it was Aristotle (fourth-century BC) who introduced three pairs of relationships to the household codes; all of which were addressed to the man. He was addressed as a husband (husband/wife relationship); as a father (father/children); and as a master (master/slave). The man was addressed because he was the one who had authority in these relationships. This threefold format was subsequently adopted by other writers.

Roman aristocracy felt that their power base was being increasingly threatened by social changes around them, with the upward mobility of socially inferior elements of society (former slaves, foreigners and women) seen as a great threat. Foreign religions, in particular, were considered to be one of the main problems, and the turning of a wife from her husband's religion was seen as a subversive ploy on the part of those foreign religions. For the established order it was clear that a wife ought not to make friends on her own, but to enjoy her

---

4 The texts in Paul where we read of instructions to husbands, wives, masters, slaves and to children.

husband's friends in common with him. Indeed, the gods were the first and most important friends.

Wherefore it is becoming for a wife to worship and to know only the gods that her husband believes in, and to shut the door tight upon all queer rituals and outlandish superstitions. For with no god do stealthy and secret rites performed by a woman find any favour.

— *(Plutarch, Platonic philosopher, 46-119AD)* —

Because foreign religions were viewed suspiciously in Rome, writers such as Josephus (a Jewish historian) used the normal model of the household code to allay the suspicions of the Romans. He was at pains to show that Judaism was not a religion that would undermine Rome, but rather enhance Roman society. Josephus made use of the household code model for apologetic reasons, using the threefold division of those codes to demonstrate to Roman society how orthodox (and conforming to Roman practice) the Jewish people were in family practice.

Paul uses the exact same threefold division that was common within society and I suggest a very strong case can be made to show that he also employs the codes for apologetic reasons (although we might wish to argue that the instructions are not simply for apologetic reasons).

Paul uses the household code model as a defence for Christianity so that it could gain a better hearing in Roman society, and for that reason to argue that there is only one model of marriage based on Paul's words in Ephesians 5:22 would be a mistake. (We might believe the comparison he makes between Christ and the church with the husband's relationship to his wife does indicate that male leadership is the only model, but we could not argue that from the household code structure).[5]

This chapter could quickly move forward to discuss what the Scriptures teach with regard to women, and seek to give a response to the accusation that Paul was misogynist,[6] and that exploration would have great value. Perhaps I could helpfully conclude this chapter with a reflection on the book I authored, 'For Such a Time as This'. It was my contribution in the late 1990s to the discussion of what the Bible outlined with regard to women. Written decades ago, I would express many parts differently now, but in re-reading it recently two aspects jumped out at me. First, the discussion was centered on church activity, with the conclusion that there was no ministry that a woman could not biblically fulfil, both genders being equal to serve. The focus (church) was very narrow. The second aspect was that there was no critique of the overall patriarchal system. I might have argued that there were no restrictions on women entering any aspect of ministry in the church world, but something much deeper is required to align church and world to the future. Perhaps I could cheekily add some words to Paul and say: 'If anyone is in Christ there is a new feminised creation'. The fall(s) skewed everything patriarchally; the Gospel brings healing to what is

---

5 Although Paul uses the household code structure, he injects them with an undermining element, that being the element of 'love'. He did not simply resort to 'order'. However, given the apologetic nature of what he wrote, we do not have to suggest that what he wrote was a description of 'God's order'. He might simply be describing an improvement on current practice, describing a 'move toward' how God wants the new creation community to inter-relate. Maybe we need to read them with a signpost that reads 'and keep travelling forward working out how to submit to one another and serve, how to love'.

6 There are many well-researched books on the biblical teaching on women. For example, the two by Lucy Peppiatt ('Rediscovering Scripture's Vision for Women: Fresh Perspectives on Disputed Texts' and 'Unveiling Paul's Women: Making Sense of 1 Corinthians 11:2–16'). I also have written on the subject and have drawn great value from writers such as Craig Keener and Richard & Catherine Kroeger. One substantial book that I would not recommend is the one edited by Wayne Grudem and John Piper, Recovering Biblical Manhood and Womanhood: A Response to Evangelical Feminism. Of course, I do not recommend it as I have a bias! I also do not recommend it as in spite of its size (just shy of 600 pages) and number of authors (22) I fail to find a discussion on 'new humanity'. Even if a successful appeal could be made to some kind of 'creation order' that would not be definitive. 'Act 1' is not the conclusion!

fallen. The critique of the world is what is ultimately critiqued by the Gospel and that is the larger issue.[7]

---

7 Another note on the release of women is to see how often in history whenever there was a 'charismatic' event that women had freedom. They functioned alongside men. When order or ordination was brought in then there was often a stance of 'only men can do this'. The freedom brought about by the Spirit accords with how the Jerusalem council worked toward their conclusion. The church would have been wiser to have followed the same path. We also need to add to this the need to understand what God is doing in the world. That too will help us in our interpretation of Scripture.

CHAPTER 3

A FEMINISED CREATION

I have in this and previous volumes often quoted the Pauline Scripture that for those who are in Christ there is a new creation (2 Cor. 5:17). I suppose in seeking to make sense of this, some older translations made it personal, suggesting that those in Christ were 'new creatures'. This though is to fail both in translation and context. Paul, more or less, simply abruptly writes for those who are in Christ, 'New Creation' indicating a major change has not only taken place internally but the whole context for life has been transformed.

I have at times spoken of a new 'world' opening for those who are in Christ, making reference to this verse in 2 Corinthians, and while that might be applicable, the use of new 'creation' is considerably stronger. 'World' conjures up an image of something that is fixed and settled,[1] whereas 'creation' paints an image of a beginning ('In the beginning') followed by a process until the whole is filled. Creation, in contrast to the word 'world', carries more of a fluid sense, we might even say an 'evolutionary' element! Perhaps we can also think of the first words into creation being that of calling forth light; light to see is so essential in this new creation that is opening. If creation is not yet the finished product, and if our context is 'new' creation, we

---

1 The Greek word 'kosmos' carries this sense.

should rightly consider that God is asking for our cooperation. If we are to be involved, sight of others is where it begins.

At the end of the last chapter, I added the word 'feminised' to Paul's new creation terminology. This could easily be objected to, and for that reason I qualified my additional adjective by indicating that the addition was somewhat cheeky. And yet...

I consider the adjective justifiable as by using it the current creation is exposed as having been shaped patriarchally. By contrast the new creation will appear as being feminised. The world as we encounter it is fallen and that is the world that is predominantly reflected in the pages of Scripture. The danger in using the term 'feminised' could be that of replacing one error with another, for in reality there is no 'male and female'. We run into the same danger if we replace male terminology for God with female terminology. To call God 'she' is no more of an error than to call God 'he', for s/he is neither male nor female. Of course, we have the male language of Scripture, and the revelation that God is 'father'. But to take such language to mean God is male (and by inference that for a human to be male is somehow more godlike and so above women) would be to err. Scripture uniformly condemns goddess worship, as so much of that was tied into fertility cults, with the sexual act being performed with a temple prostitute as being the means of stimulating the fertility of the land. The predominantly male language distances the God of Scripture from any goddess concept, but I do not see male language for God, nor even the term 'father', as seeking to attribute gender to God nor as giving any indication of a male/female hierarchy.

We also have God described in maternal terms. She (and in this context it seems pertinent to use the term 'she') is compared to a woman in labour (Is. 42:14); likened to a mother who would not forget her child (Is. 49:15; 66:13); God is even Israel's mother (Deut. 32:18); and acts as a midwife (Ps. 22:9; Ps. 71:6; Is. 66:9). Beyond those specific terms we have God fulfilling roles that women had in ancient society, such as providing food, water and clothing.[2] We can expand the imagery to include the comparison of God to a mother bird (Ps. 17:8; 36:7) or to a woman in charge of a house with servants at her disposal (Ps. 123:2).

Language! The compassion of God (Hebrew: *rachim*) is derived from the Hebrew word for 'womb' (*rechem*); Spirit is feminine in Hebrew (*ruach*). In a book written both in a patriarchal context and with such an opposition to 'goddess' religion there is a remarkable amount of material, mainly in imagery form to prevent us from drawing a straight line from male to God.

The biblical God is God alone; there is no male and female deity that engage in the sexual act and from that act creation springs forth. God speaks and there is. Creation comes from God but is not 'part' of God, for if so, we would all participate in the divine by nature. Everything we have is ours by gracious gift. We do not come to appease (an austere male) God nor to provoke the gods into activity through ritual - sexual or otherwise. God, neither male nor female, is to be engaged with, to be known (Acts 17:24-28).

In a patriarchal society where all privilege was given to the male, the head of the household, it was very important that God be labelled 'father', not to endorse male headship but to fill the word with redemptive meaning, and as we have seen to fill out the activity with much that was feminine.[3] I have no objection to calling God 'Father' provided we do not assume that gives God a male identity; likewise, I have no objection to calling God 'Mother' provided we do not assume...

---

2 Providing food (Exod. 16:4-36; Ps. 36:8); water (Neh. 9:15; Exod. 17:1-7); clothing (Neh. 9:21).

3 This was the approach I suggested that Paul used with the household codes. He predominantly addressed the one with the contextual authority (husband, father, master) and emphasised 'love' and 'respect' and relational involvement. He does not directly reject the structures, but it can be argued that if we follow the trajectory, we would not see the household codes as the goal to be attained, but a signpost back then, indicating a future direction.

We might wish to affirm that God is called 'Father' and is only likened to 'Mother', but I would respond that God is called 'Father' for that is who he is, and is likened to 'Mother' as that is who she is. We are struggling with language that holds us back from reducing God to our image and holds us into insisting that God is relational, that our ties to God are familial.[4]

OK. But Jesus was male

Making sense of Scripture is an ongoing task and is necessarily ongoing. There will always be enough light that comes forth from it to shine on to the path ahead, and as the path is shaped by what is to come there should always be movement forward. The challenge is to be able to re-read what has too often become familiar for, as said before, our conclusions can be determined before we read the book and then we can only read the book as affirming our conclusions!

Jesus as male - is there any significance in this or was it as simple as an either/or binary choice? The culture of the day would not have accepted a female Messiah, but neither did the culture of the day exactly accept a crucified Messiah! I suggest there is a cultural relevance, so that the message could be received, but we have to press beyond cultural relevance and dig a little deeper.

My unproven suggestion is that Jesus as male goes to the heart of human sin; he embodies the patriarchal, but lives differently by refusing to pull on male (cultural) privilege, and dies as a male. Likewise, I see him embodying the supposed privilege of Jewishness, and dies as a Jew. His death then is truly representative, of all humanity, but specifically of males and Jews. Those distinctives are left behind, for in Christ those distinctives do not count.

---

4 If we lose sight of the motherly nature of God, we are in danger of finding motherly image elsewhere, such as endorsing a 'Mother of God' theology, or in deifying creation with language such as 'mother earth'. However, given that we spring from the earth there is a sense in which the earth is our mother! And yet there is a sense in which creation is a child to be cared for, waiting for liberty so that 'she' can grow to maturity.

My suggestion is just as unproven as the suggestion that Jesus is male because God cannot be incarnated as female! And I defend my suggestion by appealing to what he modelled.

He was Jewish ('born under the law') but does not live in a way that endorses any idea of exclusiveness for Jews.[5] Jesus will not just gather the sheep from among the Jews, but those who are not of that sheepfold, as there will only be one Shepherd and one flock.[6] During the Passover festival certain Greeks were in Jerusalem and were asking to see Jesus (John 12:20-23). His reply to the request is interesting. The request is neither denied nor granted. Or maybe we can say it was denied at that time, with an affirmation that it will be granted at a future date. It will be granted once 'the hour of glorification' has been fulfilled and the 'seed' has fallen into the ground. His death is as a Jew but the Greeks will 'see' Jesus, the One who will incarnate God into their culture, for there will be many 'seeds' after he dies.[7]

Likewise, Jesus was male but lived so differently to other males. He fulfilled tasks that were traditionally carried out by women, such as cooking, washing feet[8] and he allowed children to sit on his knee. He describes himself as a mother hen, taking on the woman's expected role in mourning prophetically over Jerusalem. He refuses to blame the woman caught in the act of adultery, thus challenging the belief that it was the woman's fault if a man had sex with her; she being labelled as the seducer. Indeed, if we were to consider at whose feet

---

5 He, of course, fulfils Israel's commission, thus endorsing Israel's exclusive responsibility for the world.

6 John 10:14-16.

7 John 12:20-24. The many 'seeds' means there will be an indigenous tribal Jesus, an Arabic Jesus, and a Jesus representing every cultural expression. This accords with the vision of those who come from every tribe and nation. The (redeemed) ethnic and cultural distinctives remain visible.

8 Washing feet was considered such a menial task that a Hebrew slave could not be forced to do so. A Gentile slave, yes. And a woman was expected to wash her husband's feet and the children the feet of their father.

Jesus put the blame it would be at the feet of the man for, in the Sermon on the Mount, he reverses the then-current viewpoint by placing the guilt so strongly at the foot of the male even before there was any physical act involved.[9] The culture of the day debated on what basis a man could divorce his wife, but Jesus gave to women also the right of divorce (Mark 10:12).

Jesus challenged the accepted norms of his patriarchal culture and did this as a male. A 'female' Messiah doing that would have been seen as simply rebellious, and if a female Messiah had submitted without challenging the culture there would have been no redemption.

In Scripture the word of the Lord, when demanding repentance, consistently comes to the one or ones who hold the power position. We do not read 'woe to you poor!' but we can certainly string together texts that underline God's word of rebuke to the rich. In the Incarnation the word of the Lord lived among us, Jesus as that Word lived out a repentance on behalf of the powerful. His self-emptying was extreme, for he was equal to God but did not hold on to that position of privilege (Phil. 2:6-11). I believe that in a very concrete way he took masculinity, patriarchy and religious exclusivity with him to the place of death, the place that he also called his glorification. In an earlier volume I wrote of sin being to fall short of the glory of God, to fail to be truly human, and it is at the cross where we see unmeasured, outpoured love and it is there that we truly see God and humanity's true destiny unlocked. Glory is not an experience, but a life laid down that lifts up the formerly forgotten ones.

I make no apology for the direction the writing has taken (almost a discussion on the Bible and what it says about women), for this is indeed a major context that has to be outworked so that we closer align with the Pauline message. To pursue the discussion further I

---

9 Jesus says, 'anyone who looks at a woman lustfully has already committed adultery with her in his heart' (Matt. 5:28).

simply suggest looking at the many books that follow this theme.[10] Before moving on, though, I will make a short and simple comment on Jesus' choice of disciples, for they were all male.

Jesus' male disciples

The choice of twelve disciples surely was not arbitrary, and certainly not without incredible provocation. The servant that we read of in Isaiah was going to 'restore the tribes of Jacob' and bring salvation 'to the ends of the earth' (Is. 49:6). The tribes of Israel, the twelve 'sons' would be restored. The parallel to Jesus and his twelve 'sons' would not have been lost on his audience. How provocative the words of Jesus are in Matthew 21:40, when we consider that he was standing there with 12 male 'sons' and a wider group of men and women. The chief priests and Pharisees understood the implications! Jesus said,

Therefore I tell you that the kingdom of God will be taken away from you and given to a people who will produce its fruit.

Nothing subtle in those words!

Likewise, when sending the seventy (or seventy-two)[11] the symbolism is equally strong as there were considered to be seventy (or by some reckonings, seventy-two) nations. Jesus is renewing, reducing and restoring Israel (symbolised in his choice of the twelve) so that the

---

10 Although now out of print, the book I wrote 'For Such a Time as This' is available on my website in pdf format. (https://3generations.eu).

11 Luke 10:1-17. The variant reading of seventy makes the case for the symbolism of being sent to the nations even stronger. In Genesis 10 we have the list of the nations. In the Hebrew text we have 70 nations listed, but the Greek translation in use at the time of the New Testament (the LXX) lists 72. There is a scribal 'correction' in some manuscripts because the scribe understands the symbolism. Perhaps we also see a very early obscure connection to this narrative when we read that Jacob went down to Egypt with 'seventy in all' (Gen. 46:26-27). Israel has an identity, but it is for the world.

nations can be blessed (symbolised by sending out the 70/72). The servant of the Lord is restoring the tribes and releasing them to the ends of the earth.

Jesus does not choose twelve disciples as a sign pointing forward, but as a sign pointing to Israel's origins, and as a redemptive element. The choice of the twelve has no bearing on the future. They are male. They are Jewish. Both those elements point to the past. Indeed given that the resurrection appearances were first to women we might even be tempted to say that as the 'new creation' births forth there is a total reversal of anything that has gone before.[12] That though would be to create an error, for there is 'neither male and female'.

Hope for the marginalised

Jesus re-directs our understanding of God's activity away from the old perceived axis of Jew/male/rich. It is not surprising that the new community does not consist of Jew nor Greek, slave nor free and not defined as 'male and female'.

Jesus came from Galilee, known as Galilee of the Gentiles.[13] It was the borderlands, the margins. Jerusalem meanwhile was the seat of power, the religious and economic centre. He spoke from the margins to the centre. He identified with the peasant farmers, the ones despised by the elite of the city. He did not come with a powerful army to conquer and liberate Jerusalem, but in conscious fulfilment of Zechariah 9:9 he rode into Jerusalem on a donkey. On

---

12 Most male followers abandon Jesus at the cross. The women (and John, who maybe exhibited 'special needs') remain.

13 'Jesus of Nazareth' (a town in Galilee) was a term that persisted when describing Jesus, even the inscription on the cross read 'Jesus of Nazareth, king of the Jews'. 'Can anything good come out of Nazareth?' was a pertinent question. Yet this someone from the backwoods was anointed by God: 'How God anointed Jesus of Nazareth with the Holy Spirit and power, and how he went around doing good and healing all who were under the power of the devil, because God was with him' (Acts 10:38). Perhaps wonderfully ironic that Nazareth today is the largest Arabic city in Israel.

that donkey he came in through the east gate, meanwhile Pontius Pilate (as he did year by year at Passover) was coming in through the western gate at the head of Imperial forces to take up his residence in the palace. Through one gate an impressive show of military force, a reminder of Jerusalem's subjugation to Rome. Rome and her glory, visible and audible. The other gate, for those with eyes to see, a show of servanthood, glory entering that would become most visible in and through the shame of the cross. If we were to call Jesus' entry a planned political (prophetic) protest we would not be wrong. The contrast of the two entries was total, the differences stark.

Paul's gospel is rooted in the actions of Jesus, and it is no surprise that he resisted any activity that suggested there was an elite, that in Christ there was a divide between 'them' and 'us'. This energised him even to confront Peter to his face.

The life, death and resurrection of Jesus all align along the new axis of 'one new humanity'. It is for this reason I suggest he (and now the use of the male adjective is a challenge!) is no longer male nor Jewish. He is the prototype new humanity. I used to believe that Jesus rose as a male as I considered that one's gender related to one's identity, and the 'I' that dies is the same 'I' that will be raised. For that reason I formerly considered that I would be raised male; something that now I no longer believe. We know that in the age to come there will be 'no marriage nor being given in marriage', hence I have come to reconsider this. One's gender is part of one's identity as it relates to this age, but in the redemption act our identity is of being in Christ.[14] All other defining elements recede so that we 'no longer consider anyone according to the flesh'.

---

14 Neither death nor gender/sex is God's experience. Jesus tasted death, but is alive never to die again. In the age to come there will be no more death. Jesus takes humanity into the Godhead; he does not take maleness there thus excluding femaleness.

Although my suggestion that Jesus' gender post-Ascension is not expanded at any point in Scripture[15] it seems clear that all previous distinctions do not count for anything before God. To be 'in Christ' is the one factor that has value.

Beyond the scope of this volume would be to look at the implication of the Ascended Jesus being neither male nor female, into the complex world of sexual/gender identity. One does not have to agree with every aspect of a movement, but if there is a voice (a protest) that is coming from the margins, we should rightly assume that God is speaking in and through such movements. We might defend a particular position by appealing that our views accord with how it has been traditionally understood within the Christian community, but as previously mentioned we have moved on from other traditional understandings such as a biblical approach to slavery. The final word on how to be faithful to the biblical story amidst huge changes did not end with the Jerusalem Council of Acts 15. That continues to be our task and challenge. Acts 15 gives us a model of seeking to discern what God is doing in an alien world, while not letting it change Scripture, allowing that discerned activity to help us read and re-read the world-transforming message.

---

15 We do read that the vision John had of the Ascended Jesus was that he had a golden sash around his chest, and the word used for 'chest' is the common word for female breasts. Perhaps there is a further transformation beyond the resurrection and what I have suggested took place at the resurrection takes place at the Ascension.

CHAPTER 4

GOD IS IN THE WORLD

Cardinal Bergoglio (later to become Pope Francis) commented on Revelation 3:20 where Jesus is depicted as knocking on the door asking to be let in with these words:

> *In Revelation, Jesus says that he is at the door*
> *and knocks [Rev. 3:20]. Obviously, the text refers to his*
> *knocking from the outside in order to enter but I think*
> *about the times in which Jesus knocks from within*
> *so that we will let him come out.*

We have locked Jesus inside the institution, though in reality it is an image of Jesus that we have managed to contain. The real Jesus might still be asking to come in, for when he truly enters, the church will be repositioned into the world. The real Jesus prayed that his disciples would not be taken out of the world.

In the previous chapter I made the observation that we should follow the lead of Acts 15 and allow our biblical interpretation to be shaped by what we understand God is doing. Those early disciples sought to hear what God was doing in an alien culture and, by their previous definitions, an 'unclean' culture. We, likewise, should not limit our understanding of what God is doing by the poster that proclaims the latest, and greatest, church event; the event that is proclaimed as 'come and experience what God is doing'. God is at work in her[1] world, and in that sense the Jesus who is standing at the door wants to bring the world in with him when he truly enters.

I have been a distant admirer of certain aspects of Liberation Theology and, although some of it has been little more than a mix of Marxist economics combined with revolution, an overall theology should not be judged by its edges but by its centre. When I first read Gustavo Gutiérrez write about those who are 'absent' in society and explain that by using the term 'absent' he was emphasising that they were of little or no importance and were not given the opportunity to give 'expression themselves to their sufferings, their comraderies, their plans, their hopes',[2] I realised how easy it can be to live at the centre and not hear what is being said at the edges. His appeal was that we needed to hear the voice at the edge, the voice of the absent ones.

If we need to judge a theological movement by its centre not its edges, I also suggest that we need to apply the same approach to various protest movements, particularly those that have a centre that is giving voice to those who are 'absent'; such movements are asking us to hear the voice of the absent ones.

---

1 Pronouns are so difficult when we come to apply them to God. God is neither male nor female, and when we simply use male pronouns (he, his) when writing of God we are in great danger of suggesting God is either male or there is a male bias within God. I often use the term s/he to refer to God for this reason. I chose to put 'her world' in the text here simply as a small corrective to the many times I have used 'he' and 'his', and also God's involvement in the world is of a very nurturing nature, something that maybe could be better suggested by use of the feminine pronoun here. If by using the feminine we suggest God is female we would be making the same mistake of using the masculine and creating the idea that God is male.

2 A Theology of Liberation (SCM: London, 1988), p. xx.

Prior to moving to Spain, some time around the year 2000 I had a very clear encounter with the land. I was above the land and could see the entire outline of the Iberian peninsula, when what I was observing began to zoom in fairly rapidly (this was before I was used to interactive web maps, but this had the same effect, the effect was of zooming in and coming to the centre). I knew, therefore, that somehow I was coming to the 'centre' of Spain. When I got there, I came to a large square that contained two aspects that got my attention. First, a huge crowd that I estimated had to be around 100,000 people, and secondly, a stage at one end all set up but without anyone on it as the event had not yet started. I knew the people had gathered to 'hear what the Lord would have to say to Spain'.

I have written before that revelation meets expectation, and my expectation was clear that one day a remarkable event would take place where a prophet would come to Spain and address the nation in a public setting of considerable size. Expectation comes from the past, revelation from the future – hence the mismatch.

Many years later I discovered that the square called 'Puerta del Sol' is at the centre of Madrid, and from there (point 'Zero Kilometre') measurements are made. It is a wonderfully active square with many protests taking place in it or ending there.

In January 2015, Gayle and I decided to travel to Madrid as a political leader was calling for a gathering from across Spain. We thought we needed to be there to catch something of the pulse of the land, so we travelled up on Friday night to stay over till Sunday morning. Our plans were interrupted when early Saturday morning Gayle received a phone call to say her dad was seriously ill and the suggestion was that she should fly to the UK as soon as possible. We booked the first available flight which was for mid-afternoon. (We were due to be there for 2 nights, but Gayle had packed clothes for a week for herself as she anticipated something would disturb our plans.)

This then changed everything, but as we had a couple of hours before the event, we decided that we should go to the square to see what was there. By the time we left the square to go to the airport the square was packed, there was already a crowd of around 100,000. At the far end, just as I had seen, was a stage that was empty as the event was still more than an hour away from starting.

We left. Gayle left for the airport and I drove back to Oliva. We never participated in the event, though later we watched recordings on TV.

Two months later, as I walked into our living room, I suddenly experienced a major 'aha' moment. 'Gayle we were standing in exactly what I saw some 15 years ago. It was exactly as I had seen it.'

When we had physically stood inside the vision that Saturday morning, I could not see it. I could not see it as it did not connect with my expectation that had been shaped by my previous context, history and experience. My expectation, shaped by my history, was wrong! Every last detail fitted what I had seen, and still I could not 'see' it. The speaker, a professed atheist, spoke about how the clock in Spain that had been stopped had now started. He called out much of the corruption that day, and since that day slowly but consistently the corruption has been squeezed to the surface.

[Even after recognising the fulfilment I still wrestled for many months with the thought that 'maybe though there will be a future event that will really be the 'full' fulfilment, a Christian event.' Expectations! So slow to give way! I now know that was the fulfilment.]

We can write off virtually all protest movements because they are not perfect, and in doing so we can hold them to a higher account than we do the church. Ironically when we do this, we reverse the approach taken by Jesus. Jesus seemed to have one standard for society (no murder/no adultery) but had a higher standard for his disciples (no anger/no lust). We, though, are often critical of that which does not profess faith, while remaining silent about issues internal to the body of Christ. We reverse Jesus' approach when we seek to hold the world to a level of account that is not appropriate.

We should actually expect imperfection in protest movements and we should not allow the periphery of such movements to obscure their centre. We need to have a level of maturity that means we can hear the voice of the 'absent', for in doing so we are going to hear the voice of God. We have prayed for a long time for wisdom's voice to be heard, to be heard in the public square, to be shouted out in the street (Prov. 1:20,21). And for those of us who have not prayed we have sung about 'dancers who dance upon injustice'. Many protest movements that push back against the injustices within our fallen world are the very answer to our prayers.

Seeking to respond to such experiences as the one I had with regard to the public square in Spain and my conviction that the Gospel has a world-transforming thrust, I have to come to believe:

- that many of our prayers will be, and even more than will be, should be, answered by events in the world. If one of the central commissions for the body of Christ is to enable the world to be the best world it can be in spite of all the fallenness around us, then we should anticipate that there will be atheists as well as fellow-believers who call for corruption to end, who proclaim that time has not stood still, but the clock has started, which in theological language would be 'the future eschatological hope is pulling us ever forward'.
- we should not be expecting that those who do not believe in the transcendent, or have our framework, take responsibility for 'cleansing' the land or dealing with the powers over a geography or society; we (*ekklesia*) who understand something of the transcendent should be the ones engaged to change the spiritual 'climate', for that rests within our job description. We have a responsibility to clear away the dehumanising powers so that

people, regardless of faith, can rise up to speak and act toward the humanising of all people.

- that the responses of those who come through into the space that is opened up will not be perfect, and that we are wrong to expect them to be. If true authority is with Jesus, and therefore with those who are sent by him into the world, what we do with our authority will have a far greater effect than those who do not connect with 'all authority in heaven and on earth'. If we are simply critical of those who do not profess faith when they do not act in a perfect way, maybe it is our very critical response that prevents them acting in a better way!

- we need to hear the voice of God in and through many of the protest movements. They might not explain the protest correctly, and if those who prophesy 'prophesy in part' and those words need to be discerned so that we hold on to the good, we are obliged to show the same (and more) grace to movements beyond the church.

- that if we are unable to hear God speak in this way, that our deafness will only serve to skew the prophetic that is being proclaimed by the prophets within the body of Christ.

What? Follow the world?

There is often a strong reaction to the line I have proposed above, a reaction that is rooted in (at best) we are here to follow the Lord not the world, or (at worst) the world is evil and the church is God's domain. I have great sympathy with the right concern that we do not shape what God has given us in Scripture by some latest fad that arose somewhere, and for that reason we have to be continually influenced by and submersed in the story-line of Scripture. But I do not have any sympathy with the belief that God is not in the world, and that if he is in the world, we can have very optimistic expectations that there will be quantifiable evidence of that Presence. Jesus commissioned those first followers to 'go' and in their going 'he would be with them to the end of the age'. It is not so much that he would go where they went (true), but that wherever they went they would discover his presence there already.

I believe many movements that are giving voice to the marginalised have been prayed into existence by believers. Those same believers often continue to pray, and perhaps as they do there will be further manifestations and purer ones, though I doubt it. At times, though, I think what has appeared on the landscape needs to be engaged with, otherwise how will it ever become purer?

Perhaps controversially, certainly beyond the scope of these current writings, we need to ask the provocative question concerning what is God saying in such movements as we see coming out of the LGBTQ+ community.[3] God's voice is certainly not endorsing freedom of sexual expression without any personal boundaries, for the body, and what we do with it, is too important for that approach to be legitimate. Sexual freedom without critical boundaries is visible within such a movement, but what if that represents the edges of the movement, and there remains a voice at the centre? I, for one, want to hear what is being said, as well as seeking to take seriously what Scripture says about, for example, greed. If Romans 1 has a critique that includes certain sexual expressions, it also has a strong critique of 'greed... strife... deceit... malice... gossip' (Rom. 1:29). If there was a sin that included sexual perversion in Sodom and Gomorrah, I also want to hear what God says to the believing community concerning hospitality, for that certainly was an element within the original story, and the one element that Jesus extracted from it (Luke 10:12).[4]

---

3 I acknowledge the term 'community' might be suggesting that I see it as a monolithic response. I do not use it to suggest that, but as simple, convenient, (and inadequate) shorthand language.

4 By using the 'if' word in the previous sentences I am deliberately suggesting that what has been read as absolutely central might not be present in the way it has been read by many Christians. If present it is more as a 'footnote' than as the main text.

The Pauline gospel impacted the wider community. Miracles took place across regions, spiritual powers were pushed back, economies were affected, communities of believers grew up, and even those who did not personally submit to the Lordship of Jesus could see the difference that this message made to the present situation.[5] The apostolic commission does not allow the Gospel to be tampered with, but has to determine in every new situation the application of the unchangeable eternal Gospel. This set Paul apart as an apostle to the Gentiles; he had to determine what had not been previously questioned, but now was not simply to be questioned but jettisoned. For this reason, every generation needs a fresh manifestation of apostolic ministry, not primarily to forever work within the boundaries of the existing church, but to lay the foundations of Christ in situations where the Gospel has not gone before. To be effective our ears have to be open to the voice of the Lord, and the voice of the Lord inside the world.

I have written previously of Peter entering the Gentile world and subsequently opening a door for Paul to labour in that world. That is broadly speaking true but the one who first is recorded as crossing that boundary was Philip when he is sent to meet the Ethiopian eunuch who is returning from Jerusalem to Ethiopia. Eventually after explaining that Isaiah 53 has its fulfilment in Jesus they encounter water, and the eunuch asks the question 'Look, here is water. What can stand in the way of my being baptised?' (Acts 8:36). The question is profound. They have been reading Isaiah together, and they had begun with Isaiah 53, and as the text continues, we come to Isaiah 56:3-5,

> *Let no foreigner who is bound to the Lord say,*
> *"The Lord will surely exclude me from his people".*
> *And let no eunuch complain, "I am only a dry tree".*

---

5 Acts 19 with the city of Ephesus in view makes a good template to consider the impact of the apostolic message of Paul.

For this is what the Lord says:
"To the eunuchs who keep my Sabbaths, who choose
what pleases me and hold fast to my covenant
- to them I will give within my temple and its walls
a memorial and a name better than sons and daughters;
I will give them an everlasting name that will endure forever.

Previously the foreigner and the eunuch were excluded from temple worship. This Ethiopian would not have been allowed into the temple while in Jerusalem. What 'hindered' him in Jerusalem was that he was a foreigner and a eunuch. Philip and the Ethiopian now understood that all former barriers were removed. What had been declared unclean and therefore excluded was now clean and included. There was now nothing that could hinder his baptism. We can make a major error and cause offence by majoring on who (we consider) is excluded, while the real offence of the Gospel is to us when we realise who is included.[6]

The trajectory is always moving toward inclusion, and if we err we would be wise to err in that direction.

It's time to hear the voice in the public square, to hear with discernment, and to hear with a low level of judgement.

---

6 The word 'eunuch' could well have been a term used that also included all those who did not fit into the supposed traditional male / female binary.

CHAPTER 5

ANOTHER GOSPEL

Paul is considerably different to the likes of you and me! (I trust I did not hear any dissent to that statement.) The writer of so much of the biblical material that has shaped Christian faith and practice, a person who encountered the Risen Christ in a most dramatic encounter, who spent years fashioning the Gospel and its implications for his society and beyond. We gladly follow his lead. He carried an authority with regard to the Gospel and that authority meant he could describe certain proclamations as being a 'different gospel'. We have to tread carefully when seeking to make statements of a similar nature, though it seems clear that not all 'gospels' can be harmonised one with another. There are different 'gospels' and when the differences are extreme those gospels represent different versions of God, or perhaps they even represent different gods. We are to find unity with all who are of faith, but when a person denies the Gospel by deed or presentation it becomes hard to recognise them as a family member. Although we should be cautious in coming to a decision, I have to confess that increasingly with some presentations of 'truth' that, by design or by default, dehumanise those being addressed, I find it hard to reconcile the 'god' they speak of as being the God that I discern through my understanding of Jesus. If the 'gods' are different, are the 'gospels' not different? And the inevitable question pops up - are we actually brothers and sisters? Perhaps we are more like estranged family members, and in that great age to come when we will see clearly, we will see that we were both in part wrong, both advocating a 'different gospel'. Conviction (my beliefs that I hold to in the light of how I read what I read) and humility (I am more self-critical than critical of others) are needed.[1]

In 2001 I was participating in a conference in Hannover, Germany. At the end of the session in which I had shared, a number of believers from Spain came to me and through an interpreter said that in Spain there was not the history of revival such as could be claimed by the UK, and as I had spoken about the re-digging of the wells of historic revival what should they do. This was not a question I was prepared for and surprised myself when my response to them was: *In Spain you do not need a history of revival. What other nation on the face of the earth can, on the basis of biblical authority, claim to have first-century unanswered apostolic prayers sown into the land. Go dig them out.*

After the session I had to think about the response I had given and quickly came to understand that Paul's desire to get to Spain was to proclaim the Gospel in the Western end of the empire (the ends of the earth?). He was not looking for a holiday on the beach but somehow to make a proclamation in the land. Opinion is divided as to whether he made a trip to Spain. I like to think not, but irrespective, the prayers of Paul are in the land. This does not mean that his prayers are only present in Spain, nor that only in Spain can the Pauline Gospel be recovered, but that something can be done in this peninsula in order to help facilitate the recovery of that Gospel. At one level all other gospels are at best a variation of the one he proclaimed, or at worst they are indeed 'another gospel'.

---

1 Paul was passionate about what constituted the true and 'a different' Gospel but was generous toward those who preached the Gospel out of envy and rivalry (Phil. 1:15-17). We have to move forward with care, but do not have to close our eyes to 'gospel' presentations that misrepresent God. I suggest also that the essential difference between Paul's hostile response in Galatians and his generous response in Philippians is that in the former setting the result was one of enslavement. His hostility to enslavement should be our guide, whether that enslavement takes place in the name of truth, through hierarchical structure, or dominant personality.

In Acts we read Scriptures concerning the early apostolic proclamation and there are often summary statements of what they proclaimed. We read (emphases added):

*Then Philip began with that very passage of Scripture
and told him the good news **about Jesus.***

— *(Acts 8:35)* —

*Some of them, however, men from Cyprus and Cyrene,
went to Antioch and began to speak to Greeks also,
telling them the good news **about the Lord Jesus.***

— *(Acts 11:20)* —

*A group of Epicurean and Stoic philosophers
began to debate with him. Some of them asked,
"What is this babbler trying to say?" Others remarked,
"He seems to be advocating foreign gods."
They said this because Paul was preaching the
good news **about Jesus and the resurrection.***

— *(Acts 17:18)* —

*When Silas and Timothy came from Macedonia,
Paul devoted himself exclusively to preaching,
testifying to the Jews that **Jesus was the Messiah.***

— *(Acts 18:5)* —

*For he vigorously refuted his Jewish opponents in public debate,
proving from the Scriptures that **Jesus was the Messiah.***

— *(Acts 18:28)* —

*Some Jews who went around driving out evil spirits
tried to invoke the name of the Lord Jesus over those
who were demon-possessed. They would say,
"In the name of the **Jesus whom Paul preaches**,
I command you to come out".*

— *(Acts 19:13)* **—**

*You know that I have not hesitated to preach anything
that would be helpful to you but have taught you publicly
and from house to house. I have declared to both Jews and Greeks
that they must **turn to God in repentance
and have faith in our Lord Jesus**.*

— *(Acts 20:20-21)* **—**

*They arranged to meet Paul on a certain day, and came
in even larger numbers to the place where he was staying.
He witnessed to them from morning till evening,
explaining about the kingdom of God, and from
the Law of Moses and from the Prophets he tried
to persuade them **about Jesus**.*

(Acts 28:23)

*He proclaimed the kingdom of God and taught
about the Lord Jesus Christ - with all
boldness and without hindrance!*

— *(Acts 28:31)* **—**

In these summary statements of the early Christian proclamation, we do not find some of the big salvation words: justification, reconciliation, redemption, substitutionary atonement. What we do find is that the proclamation was about Jesus. When the content is expanded it might include the resurrection (the whole basis on which there is a new world order) or a proclamation that Jesus was the Messiah (when addressing Jews). The summaries are not the totality of what was proclaimed but are a description of what (or who) was at the core of what was being proclaimed. In the context this proclamation of Jesus is best understood as an announcement that the possibility of a different world had opened up through the vindication of Jesus by the resurrection. As outlined in previous volumes this was the true Gospel of which all others, and in particular the Caesar version, were sad parodies.

The Pauline Gospel

If I continue to write in this current series my plan would be to look at the biblical perspective on eschatology (or maybe better put 'my take on it'!) and with regard to that subject I have always found it strange the theology that insists on God as creator and also as the one who will destroy it all. As creator he could of course do just that, but the Incarnation (taking on flesh) and the resurrection (of flesh), and the value God places on 'dust of the earth' surely indicates that there is a wonderful future for creation. Humanity's commission for the creation and Israel's (failed) commission for the world are the reasons for the Incarnation, an intervention in order to get everything back on track.

Everything centred in on Jesus; Paul says, 'For no matter how many promises God has made, they are "Yes" in Christ' (2 Cor. 1:20). Little wonder Acts presents the summary as 'they proclaimed Jesus'. In Jesus a new world becomes possible; this new world being the current world brought to maturity, not simply through growth toward, but by a final transformation 'at his coming'. At the resurrection of Jesus a radical 'time-warp' occurred. This is not a great surprise as the Jewish hope for the resurrection of the body was that it would take place at the 'end'. Jesus was raised before the end, and so we might say, in the middle of time. Matthew's Gospel records that the event was so eschatologically significant that other saints also obtained resurrection ahead of time.[2]

The time-warp means that this new world, though still future, is now also present. It seems to be this that is behind Paul's language of 'new creation'. For those who are in Jesus, there is a change of perspective. The old has gone, the new is here. It appears that Paul is suggesting this is more than a way of thinking but that it points to a reality. Experiencing and believing that reality is to be seen in the lives of those who are in Christ and reflected in how they see others. Paul was not simply looking for decisions based on a gospel message that ended with the appeal verbalised as 'hands up all those who want their sins forgiven and to be born again'. The proclamation of Jesus carried much more weight than that, and a response meant a submission to being discipled in the values and ways of heaven. Thankfully this was more than a call to adhere to the teachings of Jesus as opposed to the ideologies of Rome, for those who committed to the Lordship of Jesus received the Spirit of God that connected them not only to a set of values but to the very life-source of the universe.

In the Imperial context of the first century those early disciples were challenged ever so deeply concerning their morals and ethics, and they were often opposed and marginalised. They knew, all too well, that, although there was a 'new creation', the old was not simply disappearing. Knowing that the final transformation would take place when the same Jesus who ascended to heaven would descend again, they understood that their (at times) small contributions were in fact like seed in the ground that would bring that final irruption of heaven ever closer.

---

2 In Matt. 27:52,53 we have a text that says that after Jesus's resurrection these saints went back into Jerusalem and were seen by many! This is a strong theological statement but there is no need to suggest it is not also descriptive of an event that took place. There were 'eye-witnesses', the same as with the resurrection of Jesus.

The expectation of this world being transformed, and the language consistently used in the New Testament within the Imperial context of Rome, inevitably meant there was a political element within the message. Not a message that called for allegiance to a party, but a message that shaped how those who believed the proclamation lived and what they wanted to work toward. If, in our setting, the proclamation of the Gospel becomes nothing but politics we can say that is not the Pauline Gospel; but when the message we adhere to speaks out against all kinds of injustices and carries the creative hope for the flourishing of all, we are indeed being faithful to Paul's Gospel.

On the road to Damascus Paul had had his encounter with the One he was previously opposed to. His previous framework of reference was totally blown away. Prior to this he could genuinely categorise himself as 'righteous'.

> *If someone else thinks they have reasons to put confidence*
> *in the flesh, I have more: circumcised on the eighth day,*
> *of the people of Israel, of the tribe of Benjamin,*
> *a Hebrew of Hebrews; in regard to the law, a Pharisee;*
> *as for zeal, persecuting the church; as for righteousness*
> *based on the law, faultless.*
>
> **– (Phil. 3:4-6) –**

From his post-Damascus perspective, he gave no value to what was previously thought as credit-worthy. For Paul, Jesus was not an add-on to his previous faith, but the means by which his faith was transformed. That being his experience, it is understandable why he was unwilling to shackle any Old Testament stipulation on Gentile converts. Everything was centred on Jesus, and he was the lens through which everything pre-Jesus now had to pass. Righteousness now came through being in him, not through being in 'Israel'.

Paul, faultless according to the law, but once he was in Christ, 'the worst of sinners'.

> *I thank Christ Jesus our Lord, who has given me strength,*
> *that he considered me trustworthy, appointing me to his service.*
> *Even though I was once a blasphemer and a persecutor*
> *and a violent man, I was shown mercy because I acted*
> *in ignorance and unbelief. The grace of our Lord*
> *was poured out on me abundantly, along with the faith*
> *and love that are in Christ Jesus.*
>
> *Here is a trustworthy saying that deserves full acceptance:*
> *Christ Jesus came into the world to save sinners*
> *- of whom I am the worst. But for that very reason*
> *I was shown mercy so that in me, the worst of sinners,*
> *Christ Jesus might display his immense patience*
> *as an example for those who would believe in him*
> *and receive eternal life. Now to the King eternal, immortal,*
> *invisible, the only God, be honour and glory for ever and ever.*
> *Amen.*
>
> **– (1 Tim. 1:12-17)[3] –**

Zealousness and righteousness previously were interpreted as requiring a persecuting of those (Jews) who adhered to faith in Jesus. Post-the-Damascus-encounter he no longer understood that his faith demanded he did God's work by making sure everything was clean and therefore pleasing to God. He now understood to do so was wrong and if he was a sinner then so were his fellow Jews and, of course, the Gentiles. But as chief of sinners he knew that God could

---

3 I appreciate that Paul might not have written the 'Pastoral letters' (1 and 2 Timothy, Titus) but they seem sufficiently Pauline in content to refer to them loosely as being written by Paul.

save anyone. As a sinner he was a blasphemer, one who took the name of God in vain, claiming to act for God. He now understood he was opposing God, as he had misrepresented the God he believed he was serving; speaking and acting for him, he now understood, he was acting on behalf of another 'god'. The 'conversion' at the gates of Damascus did not bring about a minor tweak to his beliefs and practice!

He explains that he now understood that formerly he was a blasphemer because in the name of God he was a persecutor and a violent person. Previously he had no need to ask God (as Joshua did), 'are you for us or for our enemies?' The answer was clear! However, what wisdom and insight there is in Joshua's question. Is God for us or for our enemy? If we align with Jesus, understanding the requirement to love our enemy, and even death on their behalf, will be sufficient to bring us to a place of humble silence. God is for our enemy!

The Pauline Gospel opens the door to all. Without doubt the whole world is locked in the prison of sin,[4] but God is rich in mercy. Failing to be human might bring about condemnation, but God saw Paul's activity as due to ignorance and unbelief.[5] Understandably Paul had a desire to proclaim Jesus and present the call to believe in him.

Belief in Jesus is not an automatic response to hearing about him. There is a huge resistance to this taking place.

---

4 Sin (singular) carries the sense of a power in Paul.

5 There is an irony in this. The right/wrong binary approach comes from the eating of the tree of the knowledge of good and evil. Paul says God understood he was ignorant. We can also think of Jesus praying for those who condemned him as those who did not know what they were doing! They were judging Jesus as being in the wrong, meanwhile the one in the right was dying on the very tree that they were seeking to preserve, the tree of the knowledge of good and evil.

*The god of this age has blinded the minds of unbelievers,
so that they cannot see the light of the Gospel that displays
the glory of Christ, who is the image of God.*

– *(2 Cor. 4:4)* –

Ignorance about God, for the work of the god of this age is to keep God as the 'unknown god', and the one who cannot be known, is something that the Gospel addresses. The God that Paul proclaimed was the God who saves sinners. No one is beyond the scope of salvation (not Judas who betrayed Christ, nor Peter who denied him, nor Paul who blasphemed him). God, though not human, has a human face, for it was Jesus who met Paul and addressed him personally. God, though in heaven, comes close, so close that the Spirit enters a person. Signs, wonders, miracles all being evidence of the relative ease and frequency of heaven spilling out into this world, of the future invading the present. Exorcisms breaking bondages to the god of this age, for there is only one God present in the 'new creation' age.

The Gospel Paul was gripped by started with an explanation of who this God was. Not a God that could be invented, not even one who could be found through the pages of a book, but who had to be ultimately discovered through an encounter with the Person who was the 'image of God' who truly carried glory. The response to this Gospel was one of faith. The good news had to be believed for transformation to take place.[6]

'Ignorance and unbelief' was the soil from which all manner of anti-God behaviour sprang forth. True enlightened knowledge and

---

6 In the Timothy passage that I quote, 'repentance' is implicit within it (and explicit in many other NT passages). Repentance implies a turning from, a change of direction, a mind-set change. Perhaps the change of thinking aspect is the stronger element, stronger than the regret for former behaviour. The mind-set change is about God, it is 'repentance toward God'.

faith became the soil that would produce fruit that resonated with heaven's values.

The Gospel was a leveller. What Paul counted as something that he could chalk up on the credit side of his life was eventually valueless. The Gospel did not come with a respect of status, and once responded to, any such status did not position someone hierarchically in the community of faith, hence the total resistance to Peter, and the freedom with which Paul felt justified to label him a hypocrite.

The mountains were levelled, the valleys raised. All (Jew and Gentile) sinners alike; all called to repentance, to believe the Gospel that was the power of God to salvation (to the Jew first, and to the Gentile). All of humanity having failed to attain and reveal the glory of God; and all of humanity invited to come through the door to a new creation reality, and to be engaged in a co-operative work with God within the new creation developing.

To reduce the Gospel to a set of laws; to fail to understand how it carried a vision for transformation through challenging the status quo; to use the Bible as a set of timeless truth texts; to fail to err on the side of including that and those formerly defined as 'unclean'; to consider that we are doing God's work for him; the list can probably go on. We might never be able to stand alongside Paul and say, 'we too understand the Gospel as you did', but the more we align to one or more of the above phrases the more likely it is that we have deviated from the Pauline Gospel, the more likely we have embraced 'another gospel', and the more open we will be to be defined (as Paul self-defined his previous righteous life) as a blasphemer.

Excursus: orthodox or orthopractic?

In the first volume in this series I footnoted an article by Robert Johnston where he outlined the shift in evangelical theology. A shift from a previous approach where boundary lines were drawn to bring definition, and if one was inside the boundary lines a person could be considered 'orthodox', and if outside then they were adhering to heresy at some level or other. And a shift to where a much greater freedom had developed, the only requirements being an acknowledgment of the authority of the Scriptures and the centrality of the cross as being the means by which reconciliation to God takes place. With such an approach it is indeed harder to label someone as not 'orthodox' and therefore the proclaimer of 'another gospel'; orthodoxy being a label that is attached to a set of 'right beliefs'. At one level Paul was objecting to false teaching in Galatians that had come in to bring the people into bondage, but what seemed to alert him to the issue was that of the ensuing practice that had become evident in that setting. It was Peter withdrawing from the others and it was the fruit in the lives of the believers in Galatia as they became slaves once again that alerted him.

'By their fruit you will know them' was a guide that Jesus gave and the fruit in Galatia was not one of freedom. Likewise it was the practice of Peter that was at fault. This brings me to the second word, 'orthopraxy', meaning right conduct. Right beliefs are certainly important. I might raise my voice when someone adheres to the belief that Jesus only died for 'the elect'; others might raise their objection to someone whose belief is that of Universalism. But perhaps neither camp can label the other as proclaiming a 'different gospel'. This is why I consider that alongside right beliefs one's practice has to be taken into consideration. A practice that dehumanises, that enslaves, that focuses so much on rights and wrongs that the issues of life and death disappear; such a practice, even if the beliefs are within biblical boundaries, surely qualifies to be labeled as a 'different gospel'.

In the Galatian context, Peter might have claimed that he held the right beliefs, but his practice is what alerted Paul, and in confronting Peter concerning his practice he was surely suggesting that Peter was in danger of embodying another gospel to the one that had been delivered from heaven.

Beliefs, and a variety of variations on them are probably acceptable. But what we embody, and what manifests in others as they respond to what we say, must be the real tests as to what is or is not a 'different gospel'. What we embody, how we react and respond; what we place before others as the hoops they must jump through; those are what we need to give attention to. Sadly, there can be so much hatred and insults that are generated against our perceived 'opponents', generated even by those who claim to be orthodox in their Christian faith. Love without judgement and discernment is not wise, but love that portrays the Gospel has to be one that is absent of insults and certainly absent of calling for any hostile response against others.

CHAPTER 6

THE GOSPEL WITH LEGS

I wrote the last chapter somewhat tentatively as I would not wish to make any claim to having understood the (Pauline) Gospel. Maybe what is true for most of us who seek to understand Scripture is that we have greater clarity about what something is not! I appreciate that is not always helpful, but probably a necessary step. To learn, we almost certainly need to unlearn what we have never questioned before. Likewise, in this penultimate chapter of this volume I want to tread cautiously, but knowing that these writings are simply a contribution among many, and somehow God seems to smile upon the multiplicity of the small and the richness of diversity, I submit what I write gladly.

I am somewhat agnostic about 'final salvation' in the sense of who will be present in the age to come. I think, due to the mercy of God, most who ascribe to an evangelical set of beliefs will probably 'make' it in. I also am convinced that, due to the mercy of God, many who have not 'prayed the sinner's prayer' will also 'make' it in. Regardless, salvation is by the mercy of God through the cross of Christ. Thankfully, we are not asked to make a right judgement on the question of final salvation! I do see a clarity in the Pauline writings of a community of faith and those who are not of that community of faith, but the focus is not so much on getting all those on the outside in, but (using the term 'in') those in are there to bless all, regardless of whether they are in or out. There is a trajectory in Scripture; we all probably live in 'sub-biblical' settings; the *ekklesia* of Paul's time was exactly that - it was in his time and in his culture. We have to do more than simply seek to transplant what was expressed then and there into the now and here. There are undoubted continuing principles, but if our hope is to get a biblical shape but fail to live out the biblical commission, I would rather miss the biblical shape and yet falteringly seek to align with the biblical commission for the blessing of the nations, for the work of helping the world to be a better place.

The disappearance of apostles and prophets

Most of my Christian life was spent in what was termed the 'New Church Movement' of the UK. A cornerstone of that movement was the restoration of the 'five-fold ministry' as outlined in Ephesians 4. And as the church was built on the 'foundation of the apostles and prophets' (Ephes. 2:20) great priority was given to those ministry gifts. The church was not built on the work of the priest, nor that of the pastor / pastor-teacher, but the two-fold team of apostles and prophets. The prophets could hear from God, the apostles had wisdom as to how to build. With those ministries central, and working together, New Testament style communities could be released. I am very grateful for all the influences that are still valuable to me today from that movement.

In the Pauline Gospel there is a call to honour those who carry wisdom and anointing from God, but such an honour was never to develop into a hierarchy. In our world an inevitable hierarchy has developed where churches 'belong' to a movement (or 'a stream', thus seeking to acknowledge that the 'river' is bigger than what a particular church belongs to). I understand how we align ourselves with people who bring us life, but we have to be very careful of an alignment that reverses the flow that Paul intended when he wrote of the ministry gifts.

Paul said that ministry gifts were given so that the body would mature and attain 'to the whole measure of the fullness of Christ' (Ephes. 4:13). We might (rightly) suggest that as the community has never grown to that extent we therefore need to continue with the work, and that is certainly true, but it can also obscure that we have reversed certain aspects of what Paul was suggesting should occur. The longer we perpetuate a mode of ministry the longer we will sow the seeds of immaturity. I love hearing prophetic words, and prophetic words given to individuals that restore who they are and release them to their destiny. However, if we simply continue to promote prophecy of that nature it is not long before we have created (albeit by default) a dependency culture where people want yet another word from God. Rather than connect them to God through the prophetic words, they can end up disconnected from God and over-connected to prophecy. The gift no longer serves to enable the body to grow, but ironically contributes to the stagnation of the body.

Paul saw all gifts as being present to serve. Apostolically he enabled specific communities to develop; he wrote letters to a number of them; but he never owned them. They did not belong to the Pauline stream! He confronted that whole mentality in 1 Corinthians, where they wanted to be identified with one apostolic stream or another. He confronted it head on. We read,

So then, no more boasting about human leaders!
All things are yours, whether Paul or Apollos or Cephas
or the world or life or death or the present or the future
- all are yours, and you are of Christ, and Christ is of God.

━ *(1 Cor. 3:21-23)* ━

If I were to use current language: the communities did not belong to the apostles, but the apostles, as mere human leaders, were their servants and those apostles belonged to the community. The church at Corinth was not of the 'Pauline stream', and they were encouraged to view anyone as being available to help them grow so that they might fulfil the task God had for them in their setting.

If there is value in apostolic ministry they cannot 'own' the allegiance of certain communities. In some settings the building up of the apostle's ministry seems more likely to happen than the building up of the community. The group of churches belong to the apostle and as a result the churches enable the apostle to grow to maturity!

Rather than see the emergence of the apostolic and prophetic we should be on a trajectory that pushes toward their disappearance, and by disappearance I mean from view. If they are involved in laying foundations (with the foundation being Christ) we should not expect them to be forever tinkering with how a local church is structured and operate, but to be active where there is currently no building. Foundations are laid where the building will appear whereas if foundations that are in place underneath a building are continually adjusted the likelihood is the very building will collapse.

The gift of the apostolic is to work out the implications of the Gospel into formerly uncharted territory. Paul, as an apostle to the Gentiles, had to work out the implications of a Jewish-sourced message for the non-Jewish world. Today we have so many different worlds. I am agnostic about a future one-world government, and at this point of time we do not simply have a globalised world, but also have many diverse worlds due to the fragmentation of society, tribalism and migration. Apostolic ministry has a mandate to work across the diversity of settings so that something can appear there that lines up with the values of the eternal Gospel, but is expressed in a culturally relevant way. If they, along with prophets, were to work where Christ has not been proclaimed they would disappear from sight, but their work would continue.

The egalitarian nature of the body of Christ has to push us away from elevating people, away from viewing people as kings (male or female). The inclusivity of the body should push the community of faith to be at the forefront of honouring the marginalised, of giving voice to those who have been absent.

In the world

Jesus was not simply the friend of 'ex-sinners' but the friend of sinners. He did not mix with the right people. I consider that we need as friends those who resist us and do not convert! We need them, and at times we might need them more than they need us.

'In the world but not of it' has been quoted many times, and I would like to add to that 'if we are not in the world then we are of the world'. To avoid the world in order not to be polluted is to carry the very spirit of the world. There is a very powerful interaction between Jesus, Simon the Pharisee and a woman who comes in from the street in Luke 7:36-50. Simon invites the great teacher to the meal table, and the woman enters uninvited, anointing Jesus' feet with perfume and tears. What follows next was shocking in the extreme. She began to wipe his feet with her hair. Craig Keener says,

A woman uncovering her head could be described
as nearing the final stages in seducing a man.
Jewish teachers permitted loosing a woman's hair
only in the case of an adulterous woman,
who was publicly shamed by exposure to the sight of men;
but even in this case they warned
that it should not be done with women

whose hair was extremely beautiful,
lest the young priests be moved to lust.[1]

Little wonder Simon (and we, if we had been present) said to himself that if this man was a prophet he would know what kind of woman this was. My only additional comment would be that I don't think it would take a prophet to discern the situation! It was not exactly subtle.

Into that Jesus asked Simon a simple question. He asked, 'Do you see this woman?' Simon, like us I suggest, saw no woman; he could not see past the 'sin' label, seeing only a prostitute. New creation sight, no longer seeing anyone after the flesh, is a Pauline Scripture but it was lived out by Jesus.

Our setting is in the world. In the world and not seeking to be removed from it; not seeking to be raptured out (thus opposing Jesus' prayer!), nor even making attending the next conference, that will bring about a greater level of anointing and sanctification, our passion. True sanctification takes place as we engage the world not as an outsider but as those who truly 'move into the neighbourhood'.

The world of 'self-fulfilling' prophecies is very real. If we prophesy that the world is evil and becoming ever more polluted, and therefore believers need to withdraw, and if the listeners follow that direction, it will not be long before the prophecy was indeed evidently true. Sadly, though, not true because of the prophetic accuracy but because of the withdrawal from the world. We have to allow the same love of God that brought about the Incarnation to work in us a love for the world. A love for the world leads to an involvement in the world, and then there can be hope of the world-changing. After all we are to be salt, and the salt is to be the salt in the world.

---

1 Paul, *Women and Wives* (Peabody, MA: Hendricksen, 1992) p. 29.

Of course, we have to respond to God as to where we are involved, and there has to be grace and faith as to where we live and who we relate to, but, for sure, we have to get out of our bubble of safety, of the defensive walls that protect the holiness of the community of faith. Holiness is not essentially a withdrawing from but an engagement with. Holiness has to embrace someone that is a sinner if we are to be at any real level a follower of the holy one of Israel.

We could suggest that there are two 'elements' that brought about the Incarnation. Heaven and earth. Heaven's love and inclusivity sent the Son; earth's fallenness called for and made space for the healing that the Son brought. In the same way we, as Christian community, need the world. I do not consider that there is a biblical shape for church, for just as water poured out will flow to the lower points, and where it is poured out will determine the shape the water occupies, so surely it must be with the church. The outpoured context deter-mines the shape. We might (reflecting back on a previous chapter) note that in the Incarnation God is poured out into the world that needed redemption, filling the space most in need of redemption, appearing (redemptively) as a male and within Jewish space.

I do not write as an iconoclast wanting to tear down tradition, but I do write as one who wants to affirm those who find that they cannot fit into what has appeared on the landscape through tradition. Affirm new expressions, entering new cultures; imperfect attempts, but always captivated by the love of God and gripped by a passion that we are indeed our 'brother's (and sister's) keeper'. Movements that willingly submit to the centrifugal force that sends those involved increasingly outwards; movements that are not concerned about gaining a name and increasing the numbers that sign up!

Gayle and I currently live our life in Spain. Moving to a new geography where we knew no-one, many evenings we would sit and say to each other how great it would be to have so and so living nearby (so and so being good friends who share our faith), how we could sit together on a summer evening and share a glass of wine with them. We would quickly move forward with the conversation as we realised that it was essential that friends like that were not present to fill the space. Without those friends being present it meant we needed our neighbours to welcome us. If neighbours welcome us, they (at least in part) welcome the one who sent us. It might take years, it might take decades, it might take generations for those who welcome us to find the Lord for themselves.

It is possible to make the time-table much shorter. Pick up a guitar, rent some premises, somehow get people along to let them hear the wonderful news! There is nothing intrinsically wrong with that, but we have to respond to the path the Lord leads each of us on. There is no 'right' way! There is only the path that is hemmed in by life-sacrificing love, love that is not conditional on how someone responds. When we consider the cross of Jesus we can suggest that not only did he die to enable people to encounter the Father, but he also died to preserve the 'right' to reject the God who loves them.

The multiplicity of the small, and...

I have always loved reading the stories of revival as they are so inspiring. Dramatic conversions, passionate prayer movements, reduced crime rate, donkeys no longer responding in the mines to the commands as the miners no longer used abusive language! I am ever so grateful that there are 'seeds' for great moves of the Spirit in many lands. And yet...

The early church appears to have grown at around 40% per decade. There were times of more rapid, and times of slower, growth; so we cannot suggest that the growth was always at that rate. The 40% per decade is what was experienced over a 300-year period. If we break that down so that we can see what it means. If there were 10 of us today, then in 10 years time that would be a total of 14. Ten years to have four people added - not exactly the results that mean we can write a best-seller on 'do what we do and you too will have a reputation'. If we also consider that the favourite numbers of Jesus were 'two or three', we will be deeply challenged. The amazing thing about those two numbers is that they are not four. Start with two, add one to that and we get? Correct answer is three. If we got that right we move to the top of the class. Now we have three and we add one more. So now what do we get? If we answer four, we would have to move back down again. No, we don't get four we get two, and another two.

The numbers 'two or three' are the numbers that cause growth outwards through division. And the division leads to multiplication. In the real life of people when we act in this way the division also results in diversity and it resists ownership.

I am not suggesting that there is a sacredness about those numbers but I do suggest there is something very dynamic about the methodology. Push away from a centre, allow a diversity to develop, the multiplicity of the small.

We see the same pushing away from the centre with the Last Supper. It takes place in the shadow of the Cross where Jesus is going to be taken from them, but it also takes place in the context of his words that 'it is better I go away'. Better? Who would agree with that? Yet Jesus knows that the dependency on his life being exterior to theirs could not be allowed to develop. At that Last Supper he takes the bread and wine with the exhortation that they were all (Judas included) to drink and eat of the elements. Those elements were 'his body' and 'his blood'. We can ask the simple question of the symbolism - where now is Jesus as a result of the eating and drinking? He is, and will be, wherever those disciples go. He is distributed among them. As we read earlier the Greeks will get their request answered, but not in Jerusalem, and not in a Jewish culture. The day will come when they see a 'Greek' Jesus. What other cultures and marginalised groups are waiting to see a Jesus who moved into their neighbourhood, who did not shun their culture?

The same dynamic of dispersion takes place at Pentecost. The Spirit comes to all and not to all through one of them. There is not an order of Peter first, then he lays hands on, who lay hands on. Tongues of fire appear on them all, and at the same time. There is a distribution of the life of God. Indeed, in Peter's sermon we find the continual underlining of the Spirit's inclusion, with words such as:

Your sons... and your daughters
Your young men... your old men
My servants... both men and women

– *(Acts 2:17,18)* –

Peter mentions 'all' and 'everyone' to emphasise no one is excluded, and then when he mentions specifics he includes the (cultural) margins: not just sons, but daughters; he mentions the young who are not sufficiently experienced as to make a contribution and likewise the old who could be considered too 'past it' to be involved.[2]

The work of the Spirit is to distribute the life of God, so that there can be a manifestation wherever the disciples travel. We also read that each of the groups who gathered heard those early disciples speak in the languages of those who were gathered from the nations.[3] Not only is the Spirit distributed to each ('the multiplicity of the small')

---

2 The word 'men' is not specifically added in the original text. The masculine nouns are used as per the tradition of using the masculine when both genders are included. That tradition extends to most languages thus indicating the masculine bias reflected in most societies.

3 'We hear them declaring the wonders of God in our own tongues!' (Acts 2:11).

but the act of distribution resulted in diversity ('the richness of diversity').

Revival, as classically defined, might well indeed be the experience of parts of the world, but I am convinced that the real lasting experience we should be hoping for is the distribution of the Spirit's life so that (to repeat myself!) there will be:

> *the multiplicity of the small*
> *and the richness of diversity.*

Numbers have an argument that can be persuasive. 'How large is your church?', was always a common question asked when churches gathered at a conference. The greater the numbers the more authentic and impressive the church appeared. Inevitably to count numbers a uniformity is essential so that we can count and claim they all belong to us. It takes bravery to participate in a counter-flow, as with very little to count we have very little to authenticate our choices. I wonder if we should reconsider whether the lack of real committed supporters at the end of Jesus' life should make us look for a more successful leader!

A bias toward the marginalised

Impact the rich and famous and then that gives the message credibility. That seems to be the desired approach many times in the Christian community. The Gospel does indeed impact such people, and Jesus met with and ate with such people from time to time. But it was 'from time to time'. He habitually showed a bias to the margins, and we read in Paul that those who responded were 'not many wise, influential nor rich' (1 Cor. 1:26). And from the mouth of Mary, the mother of Jesus, we read in Luke that,

He has brought down rulers from their thrones
but has lifted up the humble. He has filled the hungry
with good things but has sent the rich away empty.

— *(Lk. 1:51-53)* —

The Gospel is for all but the bias is not toward the mighty, the rich, the privileged. The good news could be understood as very bad news if one was 'a Jew, male and free'. Bad news if that was one's identity and one was committed to continue with those privileges. If willing to abandon those securities, then God would be the One who saves all who call on the name of the Lord, the rich and powerful included.

Preparing the future

All believers, and every community of believers (however tightly or loosely defined) have to be shaped by heaven's values and the context where they are as they focus on those that society does not value as important. There has to be a slowness to build, as our expertise is trained in building towers that reach to heaven, and a glad surrender, amidst the mess, to Jesus who promised he would build the church. We are to seek the kingdom with the full knowledge that the kingdom comes when Jesus comes, and we will await a fullness of the kingdom at his *parousia*. And yet...

The future, both in terms of the immediate and the ultimate future, is something that only God can put together. Given that 'the New Jerusalem comes down from heaven from the throne of God', it rather puts us in our place. God is the builder, but the materials that he will build with? Where are they coming from? Who is supplying those to the great builder? If the first creation came out chaos, what about the new? Surely those who 'see' differently should be able to supply some half decent material for God to work with.

CHAPTER 7

THE CROSS REVISITED

Paul had a sharp focus, that being the cross of Jesus. When entering the city of Corinth, he determined to have a focus on the cross (1 Cor. 2:2), and when he wrote to the Galatian community he claimed that he would glory only in the cross (Gal. 6:14). In writing this final chapter I want to briefly revisit what was opened in the final pages of volume 1, the nature of the cross, or what theology terms the 'atonement'. I wrote there of the cross being the roadblock to the path that humanity was on with no way of escaping from it. The rot had gone so deep that Scripture calls the era the 'fullness of times'. No hope for Israel, and therefore no hope for the world. The crucifixion of Jesus occurred in a specific time of history and the reasoning for that I argue is key to understanding what took place. The cross deserves a full-length book, but given that for Paul it is so central, it would be remiss of me if I did not make a few comments in a volume that is seeking to make comment on Paul's Gospel.

God does not require sacrifice

In the ancient pagan world of gods, it was not uncommon for those gods to require sacrifice, even at times human sacrifice. The sacrifice was to enable the worshipper to get in the good books of the god in question. Scripture does use the word 'sacrifice' of the death of Jesus, and the Old Testament is replete with instructions about sacrifice, but it remains that God does not require sacrifice in order that we are in her/his good books.

Before considering the application of the term 'sacrifice' to the death of Jesus it is probably helpful to take a step back and make some observations about sacrifice in the Old Testament context. There are three sacrifices that are a celebration that all is well between God and the people. The 'burnt offerings' (Lev. 1; 6:8-13); the 'grain offerings' (Lev. 2; 6:14-23); and the 'offerings of well-being' (Lev. 3; 7:11-16). These offerings are gestures of commitment, thankfulness and loyalty. Those offerings precede the others that are mentioned, the 'sin offering' and the 'guilt offering'. When we also consider that the meat offered was shared by way of eating, in the context of thanksgiving, we move completely away from a world where the concept of appeasement shaped the understanding of sacrifice.

Sacrifice can be understood in two ways, and is well illustrated in the story of the two women who come before Solomon, both claiming to be the mother of the child (1 Kings 3:16-28). Solomon's solution is to give each of the women half of the surviving child, cutting the child in two. The women respond differently. The first woman, the one that was not the biological mother, receives the advice, advocating that the child indeed be cut in two. This is one understanding of sacrifice. The death of the child will satisfy something in her, perhaps dealing with her grief, jealousy and hatred. The real mother also gives us a window on sacrifice. She is not willing to sacrifice the child, but in order that the child might live she is willing to forgo her own legitimate claim of ownership, and as a result live with separation and pain.

If we understand sacrifice through the path of the real mother's response then we will grasp the sacrifice of Jesus (God) well. If however we understand sacrifice along the line of satisfaction we will miss it. God is not vengeful, demanding sacrifice.

The cross is not seeking to deal with a legal issue but a family issue. It is not answering the demand of how an unpayable debt can be paid (Anselm) nor a guilt so great that only through the punishment of the Son can there be freedom (Calvin and most Reformed theology). Once we think family it is all about the restoration of relationships. The cross is not the transactional point in history that wins God's love and forgiveness for us, but the ultimate event of 'turning the other cheek' in the face of evil, that enables us to be delivered from all hostile powers and receive God's forgiveness, the forgiveness that has always been present. Evil, dehumanisation, is overcome at the cross.

A book (Hebrews) that uses sacrifice as the lens through which the cross is viewed makes this ever so explicit:

First he said,
"Sacrifices and offerings, burnt offerings and sin offerings
you did not desire, nor were you pleased with them"
- though they were offered in accordance with the law.
Then he said, "Here I am, I have come to do your will."
He sets aside the first to establish the second. And by that will,
we have been made holy through the sacrifice
of the body of Jesus Christ once for all.

▬ (Heb. 10:5-10) ▬

The writer makes the direct statement that God did not desire sacrifices, yet goes on to write about the sacrifice of Jesus. Before seeking to make a response to the 'yet' part of the sentence there is one more verse from Hebrews I wish to add in order to clarify something.

*In fact, the law requires that nearly everything
be cleansed with blood, and without the shedding
of blood there is no forgiveness.*

— (Heb. 9:22) —

No forgiveness without death, without sacrifice. And sadly, this verse can be taken to imply that God cannot forgive without sacrifice. There is however a process in the verse. There is no forgiveness without there being a cleansing, and there is no cleansing without the shedding of blood. The blood, in the sacrifices of the Old Testament, was to cleanse, not in order that God might forgive. It was to clean up what had become polluted. This gives an insight into the bloody sacrifices of the Old Testament, such as we read of in Leviticus. Not one of my favourite books but maybe let's jump there for a short while!

Leviticus 4 is when we have the first mention in the book of 'sin' and how to respond to it. A sacrifice is to be brought,[1] a 'sin-offering', and the blood from the animal slain was to be used, but not used to bring God around through some kind of appeasement but in order to cleanse. Indeed the term 'sin-offering' might not be the best translation, with certain versions offering us 'purification offering'

---

1 In the light of the Hebrew texts that say God did not desire sacrifice, we could also suggest that virtually all ancient cultures used sacrifice transactionally to appease, and therefore God accommodated Israel's expectation of sacrifice, but transformed it in order to give to it a different understanding than the surrounding cultures. We do not have to suggest that God instituted sacrifice. Indeed, Leviticus begins with a conditional statement concerning sacrifice, 'When anyone among you brings an offering to the Lord' (Lev. 1:2). The LXX (Greek text in use in Jesus' day) even pushes the conditional further with the explicit 'if anyone brings'. Sacrifice is culturally expected, not necessarily divinely commanded.

or 'cleansing offering'.[2] In our world it is strange to think of blood as being a cleansing element, a spiritual 'detergent' if you like, but we are not entering our world. Blood was seen as a means of cleansing (not in a literal 'detergent' sense but in a ritualistic sense), and if we continue to read the following chapters, we will encounter the 'sin-offering' again in chapter 12 where we are told that after a woman gives birth to a child a sin-offering was to be made, not made to forgive the act of childbirth(!) but in order to clean up the mess. Childbirth is not clean and we might well have means, in our world, of ensuring that the situation is left hygienic, sterile and germ-free. But the ancient world of the Hebrews is not our world, and their solution was to 'use blood' to clean it up! The solution was to offer up a 'cleansing offering'.

Childbirth, with the loss of blood, always carried the threat of death, and as the 'life of the flesh is in the blood' the use of blood to cleanse was not to appease an external deity, but to bring life to the situation. Sin, a failure to follow the path of life, brought the threat of death; the response was to sprinkle blood to get rid of the pollution.

The sacrifice of Jesus has a cleansing effect. Also in Hebrews 9 we encounter,

*The blood of goats and bulls and the ashes of a heifer
sprinkled on those who are ceremonially unclean
sanctify them so that they are outwardly clean.
How much more, then, will the blood of Christ, who through
the eternal Spirit offered himself unblemished to God,*

---

2 The New International Version offers a footnote 'or purification offering'. In Lev. 14 there is a 'sin' offering (same words as) to be made to mark the cleansing of a leper. 'Cleansing / purification' better fits the contexts in Leviticus and is linguistically sound. Goldingay, Biblical Theology (IVP: Downers Grove, 2016) says, 'This sacrifice is thus traditionally referred to as "the sin offering," but the translation is misleading... It is a "purification offering"' (p. 322). We also read in Luke 2:22 that Mary offered such an offering in the Temple after the birth of Jesus. Hardly an offering to atone for sin!

cleanse our consciences from acts that lead to death,
so that we may serve the living God!

— *(Heb. 9:13-14)* —

Sacrifice cleanses, getting rid of all the dirt, dirt that leads to death. The former sacrifices simply cleansed outwardly, the sacrifice of Jesus cleanses inwardly. The process is of cleansing (Old or New Testament) so that forgiveness might be a reality.

If we confess our sins, he is faithful and just and will forgive
us our sins and purify us from all unrighteousness.

— *(1 John 1:9)* —

The purify / cleanse word is so important, and once that is grasped Jesus' death is not a sacrifice to appease, but a sacrifice that is one of laying down rights, laying down his life in order that we might receive not simply a symbolic cleansing, but a deep cleansing.

God did not kill Jesus

In an anti-Semitic way, texts have been construed to mis-align Jews as being those who murdered Jesus. That is not the case, for 'we' all killed Jesus. The historical and geographical context, and the epoch of the redeeming nation being simply one of the nations does mean that there are many, many Scriptures that lay at the feet of that generation the culpability for the death of Jesus. One of many Scriptures in Acts can illustrate this,

This man was handed over to you by God's deliberate plan
and foreknowledge; and you, with the help of wicked men,
put him to death by nailing him to the cross.
But God raised him from the dead, freeing him
from the agony of death, because it was impossible
for death to keep its hold on him.

— *(Acts 2:23-24)* —

'You put him to death'. God did not kill Jesus, though the plan of God is outworked through the activities of humanity.[3] What a journey from the garden of Eden to the cross. On the day that you eat of the tree of the knowledge of good and evil, on the day that you embark on a path that draws lines, you will indeed surely die. Death was the result, not to be understood primarily as punishment but consequence. Israel was encouraged to choose life not death (Deut. 30:19,20) and given laws to guide them in the path of life. But they reduced those laws to be a means of excluding all others, they read the law but did not realise that the very letter of the law was bringing death to them.

[F]or the letter kills, but the Spirit gives life.

— *(2 Cor. 3:6)* —

But their minds were made dull, for to this day
the same veil remains when the old covenant is read.
It has not been removed, because only in Christ is it taken away.
Even to this day when Moses is read, a veil covers their hearts.
But whenever anyone turns to the Lord, the veil is taken away.

---

3 Other Scriptures that state this directly in the early encounters between (Jewish) Christians and their fellow Jews are: Acts 2:36 'whom you crucified'; 3:13-16 'you killed the author of life'; 4:10-12 'whom you crucified'; 5:28-31 'you... are determined to make us guilty of this man's blood'; 7:52 'you have betrayed and murdered him'; 10:39 'they killed him'.

Now the Lord is the Spirit, and where the Spirit of the Lord is,
there is freedom. And we all, who with unveiled faces
contemplate the Lord's glory, are being transformed
into his image with ever-increasing glory,
which comes from the Lord, who is the Spirit.

– *(2 Corinthians 3:14-18)* **–**

Death held sway over one and all. It was the consistent choices from the Garden onwards that led to the cross, not the inability of God to forgive without the shedding of blood. There are so many graphic examples of the life that comes through the death of Jesus. Original humanity exited the place of wonderful bounty (the Garden of Eden) eastward. Ezekiel carries a vision of a cleansed temple, where the water flows eastward, bringing life wherever it went (Ezek. 47). Wherever humanity has travelled, the life that flows from Jesus has also gone there. He appears to a husband and wife on the road to Emmaus, a small village outside of Jerusalem (Lk. 24:13-35). They however do not recognise him until the evening draws in and their eyes are opened. The re-enactment of the Garden is clear. They have left Jerusalem where death has taken place, the death of their leader and the death of their dreams. In the original garden story, their eyes were opened and they could only see shame. This couple, by way of contrast, see glory with all shame gone and their hearts burn with passion and excitement. They saw the resurrected Jesus; the original couple never saw that God had trudged eastward with them away from the place where they had allowed death to enter. He carried that death from Eden, until at 'the fullness of times' there was a concrete manifestation that it had been carried to the place where death was given the death sentence, the place where Jesus 'tasted death for everyone' (Heb. 2:9).

God did not kill Jesus, but was present in, with and through Jesus bringing the rule of death to an end. 'Choose life', was indeed his choice. Choosing life for humanity meant embracing death. Like the true mother whose choice of life for her son in the Solomonic story meant that she had to embrace death. That is sacrifice. That is a sacrifice that can cleanse.

Not just the Jews

The early chapters of Acts are historically situated in Jerusalem, hence the consistent references that they (the Jews) were the ones who crucified the author of life. Yet there are so many elements that gather together to put Jesus on the cross. Jewish religious power (the final manifestation of those who insisted on the right/wrong divide), the acquiescence of a crowd, the betrayal of Judas, the denials of Peter, the abandonment by the disciples, the Roman imperial power that controlled one and all. And we can add beyond that the spiritual powers that seem to dominate the very 'air' around us, the toxicity of a system that is not bent toward finding the path of life for people. And then we have to add the glad submission of God, who takes this all in, to end an era and open another one, a 'new creation' era.

Life is more powerful than death. Death was overcome, for it is not the equal but opposite of life. Life, true life as expressed in love, as expressed in humanising, is stronger than death. When Moses told the people that there were two options before them, that of life and death, they were not instructed to avoid death, but simply to choose life. Life could not be chosen by avoiding death; rather death would be overcome if they chose life, for in the very choosing of life, death would lose its power. Life and death are never presented as two equally strong opposing forces. God raised Jesus from the dead as a confirmation that we are no longer in our sins (1 Cor. 15:17), and in the early chapters of Acts it says that death could not hold the Author of life. There is life in God, abundant life, life that overcomes death. And as a result of the cross there is an invitation to live from that same life source.

Prior to the cross Pilate offers the people a way out. He said he could free Jesus, the one who was innocent, and bring justice to the one who was truly guilty. He presented them with a choice as to who they wanted set free? Barabbas (Aramaic: son of the father) or Jesus. Echoes of Cain and Abel. Abel's blood speaks from the ground (Heb. 11:4, 12:24), probably calling for justice. God's response in the Cain and Abel story was to protect the guilty one, the one who sacrificed his own brother. Now the people are given the choice. Yet again the choice was to kill the Abel figure. The innocent one has to be sacrificed. The blood of Abel cried out; the blood of Jesus cries out, and we hear the words 'forgive them they don't know what they are doing'. Eat from the tree of knowledge of good and evil and the result is ignorance. This inadequate knowledge, now exposed at the cross as ignorance(!), a false knowledge that leads to death, and death of **the** innocent one, is ultimately exposed in the death of the innocent one. The crowd protected the guilty murderer and sacrificed the innocent one. On that day God also, as he had done before with Cain, protects the guilty one. He does it through self-sacrifice, damaging his own reputation in the process, the reputation that he is the God of justice. His justice though is at a different level, and opens the door for transformation to all who self-identify as carrying guilt. The cross touches the mind and emotions, and in doing so can bring about a transformation, but there is something even bigger taking place where the powers that previously ruled are broken and there is a doorway from death to life (Col. 1:13).

Peter explained that life was no longer something that was open only for Jews to choose, but that 'God had granted repentance that leads to life also to the Gentiles' (Acts 11:18). Such an easy door, the door of repentance, the door of a mind-change. A change of perspective primarily about God, about oneself. A perspective that sees the cross as the place where a transaction took place, not between us and God, but between God and us, a transaction without any small print. If I come with guilt, the innocent one has taken the consequences of my guilt; if I come with shame, he has endured the shame because the other side of the cross is joy, joy at seeing the door opened for the very real start of true humanity to be expressed; if I come with a sense of sickness there can be healing for my soul. All three elements, guilt (the over-emphasis of the Western church), shame (the issue that seems to plague many Eastern cultures) or sickness (the Orthodox church) come together at the cross, the fullness of times, where they are dealt with once and for all, for it was at that time there was no hope to be found of finding a solution. We live from that time, the resolution time, pulling the future into this time and place. A firm historic foundation opens up levels of creativity and diversity.

Metaphors - no debt paid

A common description of the cross in the Gospels is of Jesus' death being a ransom for many. Behind this is a slavery image. This led to many discussions in the early church as to who the debt was paid to. Paid to God? Paid to the devil? But the language is a metaphor and is rooted in the Exodus story where the people were ransomed from Egypt (Mic. 6:4; 1 Cor. 7:23). No payment was made to Pharaoh, but the people were redeemed, ransomed. The reality is that they were delivered, that Pharaoh no longer had ownership of them, the people were set free from bondage.

Jesus does not die as a sinner

The verdict of the powers was that he was a sinner. A blasphemer (Jewish view), an anarchic insurrectionist against power (Roman view). Those accusations covered the reality of their positions. His death exposed the supposed understanding of right / wrong that the Jews had to offer, and of the benefits that the Empire claimed to bring to all the citizens. He made an open show of the hostile powers. He might have been condemned and hung there stripped naked, but truly the powers that exercised their rule through religious and social constructs were the ones being exposed.

In the section above on sacrifice I suggested that 'sin offering' should be translated as 'purification offering' and when this is translated into the Greek of the New Testament era the words peri hamartias were used. It is this that Paul uses in Romans 8:3,

For what the law was powerless to do because it was weakened
by the flesh, God did by sending his own Son
in the likeness of sinful flesh to be a sin offering
[peri hamartias: purification offering].

It is in this sense that we should (I suggest) understand 2 Corinthians 5:21,

God made him who had no sin to be sin
[purification offering, see footnote in NIV] for us,
so that in him we might become the righteousness of God.

Jew and Roman alike could view him as a sinner receiving what was his due, but God had another verdict. He dies as an innocent one, and is not judged by God. He becomes the offering that will purify all pollution. Staying within the bounds of biblical language, we can see how Paul is very careful to state that it was not Jesus who was condemned by God at the cross, but that sin was condemned.

And so he condemned sin in the flesh.

— (Rom. 8:3) —

The cross is not some pagan ritual but the act of a Tri-une God to deal in history with everything that stands in the way of humanity finding the path to truly reflecting the glory of God. It is not that my sin plus your sin plus... is put on Jesus, raising of course the question for whom did Jesus die ('only the elect?', or 'for all' and we all go free), but sin as the dominant power, sin as devouring lives, as transgressing boundaries, as scapegoating others, sin as religion and sin as division is judged in that event. Truly the tree of knowledge of good and evil does not need to be eaten from ever again. The tree of life, the tree that transcends death is no longer barred but the fruit can be eaten by all who come.

We can theorise about the cross, we can elevate one metaphor above another, but we also have to recognise that no one metaphor will fully explain what took place. I wonder whether there is something for us to reflect on in the description of those who remained present at the crucifixion that encourages us to be like them, and that if we are like them that we might then just have greater sight into what took place. The men had gone. The women remained. John remained. Maybe the one who saw love at a deeper level than others, perhaps due to his simplicity by male standards, perhaps the one who exhibited unique responses, leaning on Jesus' chest (exhibiting behavioural or emotional 'special needs'?). The heart, not the head is the means to understand the cross.

EPILOGUE

This volume is a very small contribution, among I am sure many other more competent contributions, to what might be at the core of Paul's Gospel. Inevitably the outworking of that Gospel shaped the communities that responded to the message. In all that I write above there is no criticism intended of what currently exists on the landscape. It might seem I have argued for 'small is beautiful', but gladly acknowledge the great value in larger groups with collective resources to fulfil an important mission. I am not calling for the dismantling of structures, and am very grateful for the consistent focus and hard work carried out, day by day and week by week. I see little value in criticising others; there is value in honest critiques and honest responses; and above all else being self-critical so that we better align with whatever purpose God has given to us.

I wonder how much would change in our world if we, as believers, were not hostile to other expressions of the outworking of the Gospel, but valued all who were 'in Christ'. I do think, in our world(s), the outworking of the Gospel will be much more diverse than in Paul's world, and there remains an invaluable task for those who relate together 'in Christ'. Paul wrote many letters to churches. Church continues to be important, but the shape(s) will take on a greater variety. The Gospel is eternal; the application of the eternal

Gospel is an apostolic task; the church is here in its various forms until he comes.

I dedicate this book to all who are called to work within the various traditions that have been handed down over centuries, particularly to those who do so as servants, not defending the system but loving people.

And I especially dedicate this to those who are not sure of what they are doing, who cannot produce statistics to demonstrate that they are successful. To the ones who stumble along, with self-doubt, but seek to follow the 'wild goose' of the Spirit, as they lay down their lives and reputation for the sake of others.

To the rich diversity of the body of Christ, I dedicate this book.

JOURNAL

- JOURNAL -

- JOURNAL -

- JOURNAL -

Lightning Source UK Ltd.
Milton Keynes UK
UKHW021833190521
384014UK00001B/18/J